# Historic Texas
# HOTELS

## And Country Inns

*By Linda Johnson*
*And Sally Ross*

EAKIN PRESS ★ AUSTIN, TEXAS

## DEDICATION

This book is dedicated to Ron Siemers and Charles Phillips.

# CONTENTS

# INTRODUCTION

The hotels of Texas reflect the history of the state more than any other type of public building. By examining the hotels, it is possible to trace the development of transportation routes and methods from stagecoaches to trains and onward; the pattern of immigration, architectural trends, and the availability of materials; the rise of technology from electricity to elevators to air-conditioning; and the beginning of food as an art form rather than simply a requirement for life. The change in economic importance of all parts of Texas can be charted, as well as new types of recreation and the demise of the old.

The hotels we studied fell into rather neat categories, which again reflected the growth and development of Texas. One of the earlier hotel types was the stagecoach inn. Some of the inns were rather plain wooden or brick buildings such as the Stagecoach Inn (c. 1850) in Salado, the Landmark Inn (1849) in Castroville, and the Roper Hotel (1888) in Marble Falls. Few were as large and sophisticated as the Menger (1859) in San Antonio.

Today's country inn is the modern day equivalent of the stagecoach inn. It is a quiet, restful, and often inexpensive lodging for the auto traveler. Like the stagecoach inn, many of the country inns were private homes, such as the Lickskillet Inn (1853), the Pride House (1889), and the Wise Manor (1851). Although built in the 19th century, most became inns only in the past five years. Only one steamboat inn exists from Texas' early days — the Excelsior House (1850) in Jefferson. Another early type of hotel was the drummer's hotel. Drummers were traveling salesmen who sold their goods wholesale to the general stores and various other businesses in an area. Drummers usually traveled by train. Drummer's hotels built beside train stations were the Farris 1912 (1912) and the Hempstead Inn (1915). The Woodbine (1904) was built when drummers traveled by horse and buggy.

The Ginocchio Hotel (1893) in Marshall was built to serve railway passengers. Resort hotels sprang up along the Gulf, such as the Luther (1903), the Hotel Galvez (1910), and the Yacht Club Hotel (1928). They also appeared beside the lovely rivers of Central Texas, such as the Faust (1928) and the Prince Solms Inn (1899) in New Braunfels, and Aquarena Springs (1928) in San Marcos.

Hotels were also built to serve the needs of the business community. Two hotels which come to mind are the Gage (1927), accommodating the cattle industry, and the Blessing Hotel (1904), built to serve real estate development. Possibly the largest group of hotels were the large commercial hotels constructed in cities to meet the needs of both the business community and tourists. Examples of this type are the Shamrock (1946), the Adolphus (1912), the Bradford Hotel (1925), and the Hyatt Regency Fort Worth (1921).

A study of Texas hotels reveals not only the history of Texas in an economic sense, but the history of the people of Texas, particularly the famous people who passed by, leaving impressions that lingered for years. The autographed scales of the tarpons caught by Franklin Roosevelt are still tacked to the walls of the Tarpon Inn. Teddy Roosevelt's recruitment of the Rough Riders at the Menger Bar is also well remembered. Zane Grey's visits to the Gage Hotel, and John Kennedy's last night at the Hyatt Regency Fort Worth are all part of the history of Texas hotels.

Over the years, this steady passage of people and events has had an enormous effect on the atmosphere of each hotel. They have an air of equanimity impossible to find in newer buildings; a certain sense of perspective as if to say, "don't get excited, we've seen it all, and this too shall pass." This quiet peacefulness is indeed one of the great drawing cards of Texas' historic hotels and inns.

## HOW THE HOTELS WERE CHOSEN

The hotels described in this book are ones which we chose on the criteria of age, historical importance, and current condition. Most of them were built between 1850 and 1920. A few more recent hotels were chosen because of their importance to the community over a period of years, or because the hotels have made interesting use of old buildings on their property.

We visited all the hotels in the book and feel they have something to offer the history buff, the budget-minded, the adventurous, or the romantic.

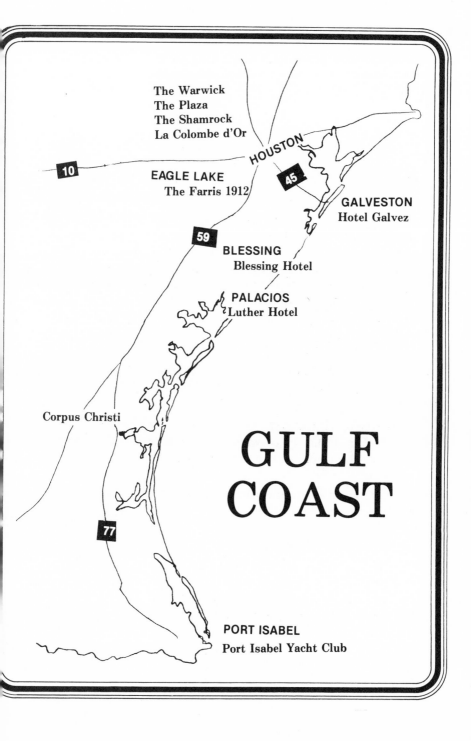

# HELPFUL HINTS

The smaller hotels and inns in this book do not have all the conveniences offered by larger or more modern hotels, such as telephones, televisions, ice machines, Coke machines, clocks, radios, newsstands, or mail and room service. All that is needed to make up for these deficits, if you consider them deficits, is a little planning. Pack your favorite snacks and drinks in an ice chest, throw in the books you never get to read, including a good Texas guidebook. If a private bath is of utmost importance, be sure to convey this to the reservation desk.

Places which do not allow children or where children just don't fit in are noted in the hotel descriptions. Rates are included in the hotel descriptions. These change very rapidly, so travelers need to check when making reservations. Travelers should also check for specials. For example, downtown business hotels often have few guests on the weekend, so they offer lower weekend rates. Resort hotels have plenty of weekend business but few guests during the week, so they sometimes offer lower weekday rates.

Bring a big appetite, as some of the inns have excellent food.

# RATES

Rates change quickly.
Please check rates before
reserving a room.

# Hotel Galvez

## Galveston

In the mid and late 19th century when waterways were the main transportation routes, Galveston was one of the most important cities in Texas. On its docks stood hundreds of bales of cotton, tropical fruits from around the world, bags of coffee beans, and sugar. The city was not only a commercial center, it was also a popular resort. Its lovely oleander bushes, swaying palms, Gulf Coast breezes, and long, rolling surf beckoned to travelers across the U.S.

Galveston had plenty of hotels in which to lodge its visitors. The largest and most elegant was the Beach Hotel which burned in 1898. Interested citizens were busy planning for a new hotel when the deadly 1900 hurricane struck. More than 6,000 people were killed in North America's greatest natural disaster, and the city never returned to its former prominence. During the next several years, the city built a 20-foot sea wall and pumped silt and sand from the bays to fill the land behind the wall.

After this work was completed, it was possible to think of hotels again. In 1910, four Galveston business people put up $50,000 each in order to build a new resort. Other investors heard of the plan, and within a month, the total amount reached a half million. The architectural firm chosen was Mauran and Russell of St. Louis.

1

Hotel Galvez

Lobby, restored to its 1911 splendor

Daniel P. Ritchey was selected as the interior designer. Hotel names were suggested: the Dixie, the Galveston Beach Hotel. Finally Hotel Galvez was selected, named after an 18th-century governor of the Louisiana Territory, Count Bernard de Galvez. The coat of arms of Galvez, including the motto, "Yo solo" (I alone) was also chosen as a symbol of Galveston's self-sufficiency.

This million dollar resort opened June 10, 1911. The "Queen of the Gulf" became enormously popular. Wealthy families came by steamer from New York or by one of the five train lines which served Galveston. They came for the summer or winter, bringing along relatives and servants. Servants took smaller rooms across the hall from their employers, whose rooms faced the Gulf.

Hotel guests occupied themselves with tarpon fishing, rabbit and bird hunting, strolling along Seawall Boulevard, or driving at exhilarating speeds of 20 to 30 miles an hour on the Speedway (Galveston beach), though this was considered outrageous behavior. Health-seekers came to the Hotel Galvez as their doctors prescribed the Galveston climate as salubrious for their hay fever and colds.

The hotel offered entertainment too. There were balls in the evening and orchestral concerts three times daily — in the afternoon, for dinner, and in the late evening. Or guests could stroll the long promenade or eat fresh seafood in the hotel's restaurant. Rooms rented for $2 daily or $2.50 for rooms with a private bath. Daiquiris sold for 20¢, a bottle of wine for $2, and a quart bottle of spring water from Poland Springs, Maine for 35¢. If guests were out of things to do, they could always drive a car on the "superb fifty mile shell road to Houston."

As the years rolled by, the popularity of the Galvez did not diminish; it grew, especially when the gambling casinos became popular. After gambling and its related activities were shut down in 1957 by the Texas Rangers and the state attorney general, Galveston entered a

The Promenade 1910

*Photo courtesy of the Galvez*

Typical guest room 1982

rather sleepy period which lasted until the 1970s. The '70s saw an increase in tourism, due in part to the renovation of the 19-century commercial section on Strand Avenue, once called the "Wall Street of the Southwest". The major renovation of the Hotel Galvez in 1979 has also contributed to Galveston's economic health.

The Galvez' renovation was initiated by the well-known heart surgeon, Dr. Denton Cooley, who purchased the hotel in 1978. Dr. Cooley has had a longstanding sentimental attachment to the Galvez. He stayed there as a child and as a medical student, and his parents spent their wedding night at the Galvez in 1916, after traveling from Houston on the old interurban electric rail.

Soon after Dr. Cooley bought the hotel, he sold half his interest to Archie Bennett Jr. of the Mariner Corporation. They decided to renovate the hotel and to obtain a Marriott franchise. The Galvez was closed for almost two years during the renovation period. The upper floors were gutted. New guest rooms were created which were smaller and of a standard size, furnished with tropical prints and photos of Galveston's early days. The lobby, however, was returned to its 1911 appearance. False ceilings and walls from previous remodelings were removed, often revealing long-forgotten architectural treasures such as French doors, elaborate wood carving, and oak beams. Bright red patterned sofas and carpets were added, as were leather and wicker chairs, brass lamps, crystal chandeliers, ceiling fans, and potted palms. Such richness and grandness make the hotel guests dressed in Bermuda shorts, hair rollers, or loud golf pants look rather out of place. But perhaps they're not; this is a beach resort and the surf rolls within easy walking distance of the hotel.

Hotel guests can no longer rent horse-drawn carriages, hitch a ride on an electric train, or race their cars down the beach. But they can rent bicycles, roller skates, pedal-carts, surf boards, and beach umbrellas. And they can enjoy all the simple and free pleasures just as the early tourists did — warm, salt-sprayed air, the cry of sea gulls, the search for sea shells, a plunge into warm waters, and an occasional magic night when small sea creatures light up the entire surf with a bright green glow.

Reservations: (713) 765-7721, or toll free: 800-228-9290. 21st Street and Seawall Boulevard, Galveston, Texas. Doubles begin at $100 nightly. Special weekday rates usually available.

Directions: In Galveston, U.S. 75 becomes Broadway. Follow Broadway until it dead ends into Seawall Boulevard. Take a right onto Seawall Boulevard.

## POINTS OF INTEREST

Churches — Many beautiful 19th-century churches.

Ferry rides — Free ferry rides between Galveston and Port Bolivar. Ferries are operated by state highway department.

Fishing — Offshore and bay party boats are available, as are numerous fishing piers.

Galveston Island Beach — 32 miles of sand and surf. Picnic shelters, campsites, are available at Galveston Island State Park. Summer musicals performed at Mary Moody Northen Amphitheater.

Treasure Isle Tour Train offers tours of Galveston's attractions.

Free observation deck at Galveston's only skyscraper not far from the hotel. Variable hours.

Historical Homes and Buildings — Being one of early Texas' most important cities, Galveston is filled with historic structures built by sea captains and merchants.

Galvez as it looked in 1911

Among the most prominent are these:

Ashton Villa — Cost was no object in the restoration of this opulent 1854 Gothic Revival home.

The Strand — One of the finest concentrations of the 19th century iron-front commercial buildings in the United States. Lined with gas lights, the Strand now boasts restaurants, art galleries, and shops.

The Bishop's Palace — Galveston's most celebrated landmark and Texas' only structure on the list of the nation's 100 outstanding buildings as specified by the American Institute of Architects. The "palace" is an 1886 home filled with showpiece furnishings.

Rosenberg Library — Texas' first free public library, contains many rare books, manuscripts, and letters of early Texans.

Sea-Arama Marineworld — Exhibits of tropical and native fishes. Shows feature performing porpoises, birds, snake-handling, etc.

Seawolf Park — Tours of WWII submarine USS *Cavalla*. Location offers a close look at ocean vessels going and coming from Port of Galveston.

7

The Warwick

# The Warwick

## Houston

If you are a member of the European aristocracy, a Middle Eastern prince, a head of state, a world-famous entertainer, or sports figure, you would stay in the Warwick when you visited Houston. Why? Because the Warwick is used to dealing with people in the limelight, serving lunch today to Gerald Ford, tomorrow to Margaret Thatcher, Burt Reynolds, Dr. Joyce Brothers, or Arnold Schwarzenegger. The Warwick understands the considerable need for privacy these people have. Employees take an oath not to discuss current Warwick guests. Another plus is that most of the employees are bilingual, and the concierge speaks eight languages.

The hotel is attractive and well-situated near the downtown oil and gas companies and less than a mile from one of the world's finest medical centers. This is one of the most beautiful parts of Houston with its streets lined with live oak trees. Hermann Park is across the street to the south, with pine trees, fine bronze statues, and a large zoo. Two impressive buildings are north of the Warwick: the Museum of Fine Arts and St. Paul's Church.

The Warwick could never have as good an advertisement as it got from Bob Hope. When asked on the Phil Donahue Show to name the place in the world he recalled as being the most beautiful, he answered, "The view from the Presidential Suite of the Warwick Hotel in Houston."

The view from the Presidential Suite, on the twelfth floor, is magnificent. This floor was added after John Mecom purchased the Warwick at a public auction held February 19, 1962. At that time the hotel was more an apartment house for the rich than a hotel. The Warwick sold for 1.4 million, a low price until you add in the 11 million required to make the hotel what it is today, a distinguished hotel embellished with numerous antiques; 18th-century French wood carvings, marble, crystal, 16th-century iron work from an Italian palace, and a 16th-century, 11-foot statue of Kwan Yen, Chinese goddess of mercy. All floors of the hotel were completely remodeled, and several additions were made: an 11-story wing, an outside glass elevator, and the twelfth floor, including the Presidential Suite.

The Warwick isn't only glitter and glamour, however. Some of its services are quite usual, such as hosting banquets, conventions, and high school proms. All in all, though, it will probably meet your expectations. Long black limousines are lined up at the lobby door, liveried doormen in tall silk hats greet you, and the lobby houses shops contain the toys of wealthy-precious stones and Middle Eastern rugs. Guests in the coffee shop discuss commodity futures or how they wish Mexico City had a Neiman Marcus. It might be fun to spend a weekend seeing how the other 1% lives.

Reservations: (713) 526-1991, or toll free from any state except Illinois: 800-323-7500, for Illinois: 800-942-7400. 5701 Main Street, Houston, Texas, 77001. $90 (double), $375 (suite), $900 for Presidential Suite.

Directions: The Warwick is located on Main Street, southwest of downtown Houston and south of U.S. 59.

Presidential Suite

## POINTS OF INTEREST

Astrodome — World's first air-conditioned domed stadium for sports.

Astroworld — Amusement park with over 100 rides, shows, and attractions.

The Galleria — Shopping center containing a variety of shops and restaurants.

Hermann Park Zoo — Large, interesting zoo, includes a children's petting zoo.

Port of Houston — Among three top seaports in the U.S. in tonnage. Free tour boat ride and observation area.

Restaurants — Hundreds of outstanding restaurants. *Houston City Magazine* offers dependable reviews.

San Jacinto Battleground State Historic Park — Site where Texas won independence from Mexico in 1836. Battleship *Texas* is moored in park.

Texas Medical Center — Immense complex of hospitals, medical schools, and research institutions.

NASA — Tours available at this space exploration center.

The Plaza

. . . Comfort with class

# The Plaza

## Houston

The Plaza is the only hotel in Houston which still has traces left of another era. Part of this is due to the fact that it was not built as a standard commercial hotel, but with the roomy accommodations of an apartment hotel. This was something new for Houston, even though there were similar types of hotels in the Northeast and Europe. The grand opening advertisement that Sunday, February 21, 1926, read:

> Visitors will be welcome throughout the afternoon and again in the evening, when the entire building may be inspected under a myriad of electric lights. Built to meet the demands of present day living, brought about largely by the advent of the motor vehicle, the Plaza may be termed a transient-family hotel, embracing as it does all the comforts of a modern home, with the many conveniences of the high class hotel.

There were twin or double Murphy beds with Sealy mattresses in every bedroom, maid service, 9½-foot ceilings, ceiling fans, louvered doors, extra maids available for parties, both hot and ice water, linens, china, and silverware. The kitchen had a Kenerator for waste disposal and had extra ventilation to keep the apartments as cool as possible. All apartments had furniture custom made by Albert Pick and Co. in Chicago. Most of

13

the furniture is still in the rooms, but the Murphy beds have almost all been removed.

The lobby was decorated with tapestries, draperies, rugs, and vases of the Italian Renaissance period. To the left of the lobby, where the library now is, there was a ladies' parlor decorated in Venetian style. To the right was the barbershop. The dining room was decorated with Portuguese furnishings. In the basement was the commissary, with its stores of fruits, vegetables, and meats. It was advertised as a service for the busy housewife who could order over the phone, have deliveries made to her kitchen entrance, and charged to the monthly bill.

The building is in the American Renaissance design, of reinforced concrete, faced with brown tapestry brick, ornamental stone, and terra cotta trim. The two wings are at a slight angle to the central core, so the shape is that of a relaxed C. It sits diagonally on the block to get the maximum southeast exposure. The architect was Joseph Finger, who also designed Houston's City Hall. A 120-foot veranda ran the full length of the building to catch the Gulf breezes in the hot summer months. A new concession to the beginning automobile age is the two-story Plaza garage, similar in architectural design to the hotel.

The Plaza has had several owners, particularly in recent years. Twenty years after being built, it was closed and then purchased by the J.H. Kurth family, who retained ownership for 25 years. Since being sold in 1970, there have been at least four owners. However, the Plaza's essential character perseveres in spite of changes. This sense of permanence is one of the endearing qualities of the Plaza. Fifty-five years ago it was a hotel for overnight guests and apartment dwellers. Today the situation is still the same, except that there are fewer apartments. Some of the same apartment renters, predominantly older women, have lived here for years.

Now there are also young professionals who make the Plaza their home.

The surrounding area has not changed much either. Advertised originally as being "in the heart of the city's most aristocratic section, nesting midst the Museum of Fine Arts, the Rice Institute, and the rich and exclusive homes of Shadyside," the atmosphere is still that of art museums, universities, gracious older homes, churches, and tree-lined streets. Much of the Plaza's atmosphere comes from its surroundings, and in fact, some people refer to it as the art hotel. It has become a rather stylish place to live.

With all of Houston's frenetic activity, it is easy to forget that the young city has a past. The Plaza is a perfect embodiment of the new and the old — in its inhabitants, its accommodations, and its spirit.

Reservations: 713-524-3161, 5020 Montrose Boulevard, Houston, Tx 77006. $55 up for doubles, $60 to $200 for suites.

Directions: The Plaza is south of downtown Houston near the Medical Center, Rice University, and Hermann Park.

POINTS OF INTEREST

See the Warwick.

15

The Shamrock Hilton

# Shamrock Hilton

## Houston

The Shamrock Hotel was built as the symbol of one man's gratitude for the city and state which had done so much for him. Glenn McCarthy started his adult life pumping gasoline. With some good judgment and good luck, he found himself a Texas oil multimillionaire in his thirties. There seemed to be no end to his good fortunes, which gave him a growing urge to do something for the city and state of such unlimited opportunity. He wanted to do something which would really put Houston on the map. He decided to build a Texas-size hotel.

He was far-thinking in his plans for this hotel. It was to be a convention hotel, a type which would be badly needed in Houston's future. A believer in decentralization, he built it several miles from the downtown businesses even though people warned him that it could never succeed sitting so far out on the prairie. They were wrong, of course. The hotel has been a success since it opened on St. Patrick's Day in 1949.

The Shamrock is hardly old enough to be classified as one of Texas' historic hotels, yet it is included because of its importance to the community over the years. For many years there were few tall buildings in the area, which made the 18-story, 1000-room hotel with a green roof and a huge American flag flown at the top rather conspicuous.

The hotel's opening days were so wildly flamboyant they seem incredible, even though well-documented by

17

The Terrace

photos in many newspapers and magazines. Some say the opening was the biggest drunken brawl ever seen. Others say it was a most exciting high society party. One newspaper possibly described it best by calling it "an event of rip-snorting chic as only a Texas wildcatter could produce".

McCarthy invited over 2,000 guests to the hotel's opening and the premier showing of a movie he produced about America, "The Green Promise". Guests from the East Coast and Midwest were flown in. Movie stars from the West Coast arrived by a train dubbed "the Shamrock Special". As the train pulled into Union Station, the world's press awaited the stars: Laurel and Hardy, Walter Brennan, Gale Storm, Kirk Douglas, Edgar Bergen, Rhonda Fleming, and Robert Stack.

Writers, business tycoons, and political figures were everywhere. McCarthy, proud Irishman that he was, had 2,000 shamrocks flown in from Ireland to hand out as boutonnieres. Orchids were also distributed. A fine steak dinner was somehow served through the melee.

Ted Mack brought his Original Amateur Hour to town in honor of the occasion and Dorothy Lamour broadcast her NBC radio show over the air from the Emerald Room. Her guests were Errol Flynn and Glenn McCarthy. Twelve floodlights and eight searchlights lit the night; the Shamrock could be seen for miles. As the newspapers put it, for one night, the Shamrock became the social center of the world. It had seemed more like fiction than fact. No wonder it inspired the hotel scenes in Edna Ferber's *Giant.*

Although the hotel flourished, McCarthy ran into financial problems and sold the Shamrock to Conrad Hilton in 1954. From that time on it has been called the Shamrock Hilton.

The Shamrock cost $21 million to construct, and the building supplies required were mind-boggling: 690 carloads of sand and gravel, 190 carloads of cement, 2100 tons of reinforced rods, 100 carloads of brick, 140 carloads of tile, 125 carloads of mortar, and ten acres of carpeting. The hotel is still considered large by any standards. On its 15-acre grounds are tennis courts and the world's largest hotel swimming pool, the size of a football field, and surrounded by green lawns and tall palm trees.

The hotel has every possible service plus Neiman Marcus and Sakowitz shops, a Persian carpet shop, and a jeweler. Airline and car rental agencies are well represented. The hotel's banquet rooms and exhibit halls remain among the nation's largest. The rooms are pleasantly decorated, and the lobby, with its rose travertine columns, Honduras mahogany walls, and enormous chandeliers, is attractive.

The Shamrock's days as an extravagantly Texas hotel have not ended. Each May, the Shamrock Hilton hosts the Western Heritage Sale. Ranchers and the oil-rich come to purchase the very finest quarter horses, Angus, and Charolais cattle, or to bid on Western paintings or sculpture. The livestock is housed on the Shamrock grounds, and visitors are invited to look at animals worth $25,000 and up. If you want to attend the livestock or art auction held inside the hotel, be ready to pay a hefty fee just for the privilege of bidding. It might be worth it, though, to get to sit by John Connally or someone from the King Ranch.

Reservations: (713) 668-9211. 6900 Main, Houston, Texas 77030. $76 up for doubles.

Directions: The Shamrock Hilton is located three miles southwest of the downtown area, at the intersection of Holcombe and South Main.

POINTS OF INTEREST

See Points of Interest for the Warwick.

# La Colombe d'Or

## Houston

Steve Zimmerman bought the old Fondren Mansion in 1978, intending to tear it down and build high-rise condominiums. Instead, he saw potential in creating a hotel and restaurant, La Colombe d'Or, patterned after its namesake, an inn on the Riviera in France. The original La Colombe d'Or was built around the turn of the century and had guests such as Chagall and Modigliani who exchanged their art for meals and lodging.

The Fondren was an excellent choice for recreating La Colombe d'Or. It is large enough to serve as a small hotel, yet it retains the feeling of a private home. The massive 21-room Fondren Mansion was designed in 1923 by Alfred C. Finn for Walter Fondren, one of the founders of Humble Oil Co., now part of the Exxon Corporation. Finn also designed several Houston-area structures: the San Jacinto monument, the Gulf Building, St. Paul's Church, and one wing of the Rice Hotel. Mr. Fondren died in 1939, but Mrs. Fondren continued to live there until 1949, when she granted the property to the Visiting Nurse Association of the Red Cross free of rent for 30 years.

After Steve purchased the property in 1979, he renovated the building with assistance from the Zeta Tau Alpha sorority, which used it for its annual designer showcase. Linoleum which had been put down over hardwood floors was ripped out. Acoustical tile was removed to reveal molded ceilings. A parquet floor of maple,

La Colombe D'Or

cherry, mahogany, and oak was installed in the entry way. A carved walnut bar was created from separate pieces imported from England and Scotland.

After the show, some rooms were redone, particularly the guest rooms. They are sumptuously decorated with Oriental rugs, art work, antiques, and king-sized beds with firm mattresses. The rooms have their own private dining rooms which were formerly sleeping porches or sun rooms. The bathrooms have tile floors and brass faucets. Instead of being numbered, the rooms are named Monet, Degas, Renoir, Van Gogh, or Cezanne.

Each guest receives fresh flowers, a decanter of brandy, a plate of fresh fruit, a box of mints, shampoo, Devon violet soap, a bathrobe, the *Wall Street Journal, New York Times,* or other newspaper, and a continental breakfast of fresh orange juice and hot croissants. Meals in the individual dining rooms are not limited to items on the menu. Another amenity is access to a Mercedes Benz with driver.

The third-floor penthouse opened in the fall of 1981 in what used to be a ballroom, and there are plans to open a French bakery soon on the first floor. La Colombe d'Or is a place to consider for a special occasion, or just for feeling rich and pampered.

Reservations: 713-524-7999, 3410 Montrose, Houston, Tx 77005. $200 for rooms, $500 for penthouse. Ask about corporate rates.

Directions: La Colombe d'Or is a mile southwest of downtown Houston.

POINTS OF INTEREST

See the Warwick.

The Farris 1912

Bently-Farris House

# The Farris 1912

## Eagle Lake

In 1857 the Good Hotel was built by Gamiel Good on the same site as the present-day Farris 1912. It was a two-story wooden structure with front porches facing the Houston-San Antonio Road. When the railroad arrived, it was only a few yards from the front of the hotel. The rooms were 8' by 10' and frugally furnished with one bed, one chair, a nail to hang clothes on, and a tin basin on an old soap box in the corner for washing. The partition walls were constructed of pine boards, which were not papered, painted, or planed. The boards had shrunk, leaving large cracks.

In 1906, the Good Hotel was sold to W.A. Dallas. The old building was demolished, and a new brick building was built in 1912. A.E. Barnes of Houston was the architect. He was a well-known architect who designed the home which became the administration building of the University of St. Thomas, and the Courtland Place homes in Houston. The new hotel, named the Hotel Dallas, was built with red brick exterior walls of 18-inch construction. The interior contained velvet draperies and ceiling fans with clusters of lights. It also had running water and indoor sanitary facilities, which were a great novelty at that time.

The hotel was designed with a central solarium around which the lower rooms radiate. The second floor contained six bathrooms, multiple skylights, and bedrooms with broad windows. It was a very fine hotel for a small Texas town. In the years that followed, the elegant Hotel Dallas was the center of the town's business and social life.

The hotel was sold to various owners, including the Ramseys, who renamed it the Hotel Ramsey. The Hotel Ramsey suffered greatly during the Depression and continually declined with the demise of passenger rail and the rise of the motor hotel with its private baths and television sets. The Hotel Ramsey eventually reached a state of pitiful disrepair, and its clientele became the down-and-out people in need of cheap beds. It was at this stage in the hotel's history, in 1974, that Helyn and Bill Farris bought the hotel.

Its floors were eaten by termites, the rooms were waist-high in trash, the curtains and walls were covered with cockroaches, and the mattresses were cigarette-burned. The Farrises spent many 18-hour days and 7-day weeks the next four years restoring the building they had admired for many years. They rewired and replumbed the building, painted, installed new floors, and refinished the woodwork. They removed partitions, returning the building to its original room division. The staircase was returned to its original place under a large skylight.

The result of their work is spectacular. The hotel is now very elegant with its Victorian-style carpet and Nottingham lace and satin draperies. Helyn's florist background is evident in the beautiful, healthy plants which are placed throughout the hotel.

The bedrooms are on the second floor. Each room is decorated differently: all have antique furnishings, some of which were salvaged from the original furniture. A few of the rooms contain sinks, others have ceramic wash bowls. There are restroom facilities on the floor for rooms without baths. Many of the room furnishings are for sale.

When the restoration was completed in 1977 one year ahead of schedule, its main patrons were no longer train travelers or itinerant salesmen, but hunters. Eagle Lake calls itself the goose hunting capital of the world. In the fall, the town is visited by duck and geese hunters who enjoy staying in the beautiful Farris 1912. Few motels can compete with the Farris for good service and delicious food. Bill gets up at 4 a.m. to prepare a big breakfast. Coffee is prepared for the hunters' thermos bottles, and their dirty shoes are cleaned at night. The Farrises can arrange for hunting guides. Three meals daily are included in this special hunter's package.

With the restoration of the Bentley-Farris House next door, the hotel now serves not only hunters in the winter, but can accommodate travelers at any time. This structure was built in the 1920s as a boarding house and was run by a Mrs. Calvert. Her father financed the construction, so it was named after him. Winthrop Rockefeller stayed there with a friend in the 1930s for six months when he was sent to the area to learn the oil business. The boarding house meals were open to the townspeople. In the 1940s it was turned into an apartment building and remained so for the next thirty years. There are eight rooms which can be rented as rooms or as suites. Each suite has its own parking place in front of the door and a separate entrance.

After hunting season, the price includes only a breakfast of homemade rolls and coffee. Meals are served seven days a week with reservations, except Christmas. The food is very well prepared. It is worth the trip to the hotel just for the food and browsing in the hotel's antique and flower shop or strolling around the hotel looking at more antiques.

Reservations: 713-234-2546, 201 N. McCarty, Eagle Lake, Tx 77434. Winter hunter's package plan — $50/day per person based on double occupancy, 50% deposit required. Regular guests—single $30, double $40. No pets. Children under 12 not accepted.

Country Inn Elegance

Directions: Eagle Lake is on U.S. 90-A, approximately 50 miles west of Houston. The Farris 1912 is located across the railroad tracks in the downtown area.

## POINTS OF INTEREST

Attwater Prairie Chicken National Wildlife Refuge. Headquarters may be reached by traveling northeast from Eagle Lake on F.M. 3013 for six miles to the refuge sign entrance.

28

# *Blessing Hotel*

## *Blessing*

At 6 a.m. each day, the Blessing Hotel opens. Within minutes its tables are taken by ranchers, rice farmers, and oil field workers ready for some solid sustenance that will carry them through the morning's labor. The menu offers steak, sausage, ham, bacon, hot cakes, fried eggs, grits, toast, and coffee. Patrons serve their own coffee and wander into the kitchen to see how breakfast is going. Stories are swapped and gossip exchanged. A newspaper is not needed to find out what happened the night before, whose cattle was hit by lightning, or whose barn burned down.

When this group leaves, all will be quiet except for the occasional neighbor or traveler who comes by for breakfast or just a cup of coffee, paid for on the honor system.

Sundays are even busier, with visitors from as far away as Houston partaking of the Blessing Coffee Shop's beef tips, fried fish from the nearby Gulf, chicken-fried steak, homemade noodles, greens, cornbread, and rolls. Lunch is served buffet style. The food is taken to rough but sturdy wood tables covered with red and white checked plastic cloths.

The dining room is quite plain and bare, with 10-foot ceilings, wood floors, and ceiling fans which take off some of the summer's heat. The dining room was once the hotel's ballroom.

Next to the dining room are two guest rooms which

Blessing Hotel

have been decorated to look as they did in the early 1900s. There are no plans to air-condition or supply central heat to the rooms, as that would take away from the hotel's authenticity. At least that is the thought of the Blessing Historical Association, which now owns the hotel. Other rooms, 25 in all, will eventually be remodeled and furnished with period furnishings as funds from the association allow. They are hoping visitors to the hotel will contribute to the hotel's renovation.

The Blessing Hotel was built in 1906 by the town's founder, Jonathan Pierce. Jonathan came to Texas in 1859 to seek his fortune and to join his brother Abel, better known as Shanghai Pierce. The two men punched cattle and worked their way up to being wealthy landowners. Jonathan founded the town of Blessing and named it in 1903. That was the year the railroad reached Blessing. Jonathan was so thrilled at the arrival of the railroad that he decided to give the town a name—Thank God. The post office could not agree to that, so he named it Blessing.

Jonathan Pierce had the Blessing Hotel built the following year. The building is interesting, Spanish mission in style, yet built of wood rather than adobe and stucco. For this reason the hotel was once called the Alamo de Blessing. The hotel's first clients were the real estate developers who came to Blessing by train in hopes of convincing potential buyers of the area's possibilities for fruit tree farming.

The Blessing Hotel has served as a hotel since it was built, except from 1972 to 1978, when it was closed. The Pierce family gave the hotel to the Blessing Historical Association with the stipulation that the Pierces maintain control over renovation plans. The Historical Association has begun painting, cleaning, and repairing the building. The end result is a hotel that is plain and simple, friendly, and relaxed.

Reservations: (512) 588-6623. $15 to $17 daily, $40 to $60 weekly. Not all rooms have baths. No air-conditioning.

Directions: Blessing is located on Texas 35, approximately 100 miles southwest of Houston. The Blessing Hotel is in Blessing on Texas 35.

## POINTS OF INTEREST

Gravestones of Shanghai and Jonathan Pierce in cemetery, 1 mile east of Blessing.

Matagorda County Museum—Bay City—early Texas clothing, furniture, maps.

See Points of Interest for Luther Hotel in Palacios.

# Luther Hotel

## Palacios

When we arrived at the Luther Hotel late one summer night, several guests were sitting in the lobby watching the hotel's one television set. Mrs. Luther
remembered our names and room number without checking her schedule. Handing us several thick towels in case
we needed extras, she pointed us toward our room
without asking us for identification or payment. With
this welcome, it did not take long to feel at home.

The Luther Hotel, built in 1903, was called the Old
Palacios Hotel. It was built on East Bay Front to serve
the many visitors from the North and East who came to
invest in the lands, orchards, and homes of the Gulf
Coast. This was a boom period along the coast, and in
1905 the hotel was moved to its present location and
enlarged to accommodate the tourist trade which had
become heavy during the summer and winter seasons.
The Old Palacios Hotel became the center of the cultural
and social life of the area.

The present owners bought the hotel in 1938, renaming it the Luther Hotel. It now functions less as a fancy
resort and more as a winter home for retired people from
all over the U.S. and Canada. Its two-and-three-bedroom
apartments are comfortably furnished and overlook Tres
Palacios Bay.

The winter guests, many of whom have been coming
to the hotel for 10 to 15 years, are all part of the Luther
Hotel family and socialize together almost every even-

Luther Hotel

ing. They go to the game room for coffee, tea, and cake; they play bridge and canasta; show slides and movies of their world travels; sing, and play the piano. Mrs. Luther told us that of the guests there is an excellent pianist from Minnesota, one from Missouri, and an Italian tenor. On some evenings the guests prepare a meal for everyone which is made up of specialties from their states and countries.

The Luther Hotel is not just a winter home for escapees from the cold North, however; it is also a year-round get-away-from-it-all place for fishing and quiet walks down the bay road. The hotel does not have television, radios, or telephones in the rooms. Instead, visitors listen to the sounds of the waves rolling on the shoreline, the wind whispering through the palm trees, and each other. Hunters arrive in the fall to hunt duck and geese on the rice marshes around Collegeport. Long term visitors told us that the fishing is good; in the fall, trout can be caught from the end of the pier.

We had made reservations for the motel courts located on the hotel grounds because it was summer, and the hotel rooms are not air-conditioned. However, after seeing the hotel rooms, we realized they have been quite comfortable because of the high ceilings, ceiling fans, and large windows that open toward the bay. Each court contains a fully furnished kitchen, (dishes, towels, cooking utensils), a living room, bathroom, and bedroom. It was nice to be able to keep cold drinks, cheese, and fruit in the refrigerator and to heat up coffee and rolls in the morning. With so many conveniences, the court felt more like a home or beach house, especially since the courts have castoff and mismatched furniture which contribute to the homey atmosphere.

All rooms face the bay. The beds are comfortable, and the high ceilings lend an air of spaciousness. The rooms have been kept in good repair but have not been completely restored and refurbished, so you can easily get the feeling of being in an earlier time. The Luther

The Luther's "Gallery" — A winter haven

seems to invite wandering and exploration. There are nooks and crannies, a TV area, recreation room with a coffee pot always on, and books from hallway bookcases to read.

It is difficult to look at this section of the Gulf Coast and not think about the hardships faced by the explorers and settlers of the "fever coast". In fact, only 25 miles from the Luther Hotel is a statue of La Salle, the famous French explorer, solemnly facing the sea near the spot where he came ashore almost 300 years ago. La Salle set out in 1684 to establish a fort at the mouth of the Mississippi River. The army for this ill-fated expedition was made up of "30 gentlemen adventurers from France, three friars, three priests, some girls seeking husbands, and a hundred or so men dragged out of taverns."

During the voyage, one ship was sunk by the Spaniards, and one was wrecked on the Gulf Coast. The remaining two ships landed at Matagorda Bay, missing the voyagers' destination by 400 miles. A wooden stockade was built and named Fort St. Louis. A worse site could not have been chosen. The low, marshy land was unhealthy for this party already weakened by tropical diseases. Fort St. Louis was in the heart of Karankawa Indian country.

With supplies running low, La Salle left the fort with a few able-bodied men to seek help from other French forts near the Mississippi River. On the march, some of the men mutinied, killing La Salle from ambush. Meanwhile, smallpox had broken out at Fort St. Louis. The male survivors of the smallpox epidemic were killed by the Karankawas, and women and children were carried off to the Karankawa villages. La Salle's statue, facing the ocean, is an appropriate representation of the far-sighted and visionary qualities which were necessary to settle this land.

Reservations: (512) 972-2312. South Bay Blvd., P.O. Drawer V, Palacios, Texas 77465. Hotel apartments must be rented for a minimum of three months in winter, $185 to $200 monthly; long-term guests must make application in person. Hotel rates are $14 up; rooms are not air-conditioned. Motel courts are $30 per night, are air-conditioned, have fully furnished kitchen, sleep four.

Directions: Turn left at the first red light when entering Palacios from the east on Texas Highway 35.

## POINTS OF INTEREST

Three free lighted fishing piers, public boat ramps, small camping areas.
Marine Fisheries Research Station
Matagorda County Museum, early Texas artifacts, in Bay City.
Magnolia Beach, near Indianola, swimming, sailing.
Aransas Wildlife Refuge, near Rockport, winter home of the whooping crane.
Padre Island National Seashore.

# Yacht Club Hotel

*Port Isabel*

The name of this hotel brings up images of a high-class private club with a doorman to greet arriving guests. In reality it is a relaxed, casual place, open to the public, where surfers stay because it is near Padre Island and inexpensive, where families stay because it's such a delightful change from chain motels, and where local people come dressed in their Sunday best to eat at the hotel's fine restaurant.

The Yacht Club Hotel was a private club when it opened in 1928. It was built by a corporation to serve about 200 members. When the Depression came one year later, the club folded. Mr. Shary from the Rio Grande Valley bought out the other members and opened the hotel to the public. It gradually deteriorated and was closed in 1969. Bud Franke and Sons, Realtors, purchased it in 1970, restored it, and then opened it to the public again.

The Yacht Club is quite attractive. It has a Spanish look — white stucco walls and a red tile roof. The palm trees and oleander bushes add to its tropical flavor. It is a casual place with no bellboys or room service for its 26 rooms, but what services do you need when your plans are to take trips to the beach, eat seafood in the downstairs dining rooms, or travel across the border to Mexico?

Speaking of seafood, the hotel restaurant is quite good. It has a relaxed atmosphere, which makes it a nice

Yacht Club Hotel

place for a long, slow dinner, and the suits and ties worn by some guests add a touch of elegance. Seafood is the main item on the menu which includes oysters, redsnapper, crab, shrimp, scallops, lobster, and trout. The fried food is deliciously prepared in a light batter, the salad and soup are fresh, the service is good, and there is a good variety of wine and bar drinks.

The hotel rooms are comfortable but have an early 1960s look. There are shag carpets, brown paneling, and a television. The accessories, such as Mexican bark paintings, are simple, however, and create a plain and pleasant atmosphere. There are plenty of deck chairs on the veranda running in front of the rooms, great for visiting or sunset watching. The biggest drawback to the rooms is their thin walls.

If you visit the Yacht Club Hotel, you'll find plenty of things to do in and around Port Isabel. Fishing trips are available right across the street from the hotel. There is a batik factory in Harlingen, the Gladys Porter Zoo in Brownsville, mile after mile of citrus farms and several flea markets and roadside peddlers on the road to McAllen. South Padre Island is nearby with its white beaches and sand dunes. It has become built up with many high-rise hotels and condominiums, but the farther you drive into the interior of the island, the more the buildings begin to thin.

A trip to Matamoros should be included in a stay at the Yacht Club Hotel. After driving to Brownsville, catch a taxi from the Mexican side of the bridge or walk about 10 blocks to the Artesenal Central, a government-sponsored arts and crafts shop. It has pottery, textiles, wood, and jewelry from all over Mexico, with no bargaining and reasonable prices. If you prefer the excitement of the market place, you can also walk or take a taxi. You may just want to walk around and absorb the flavor of a very different city.

The Yacht Club Hotel is a desirable combination of pleasant surroundings, a relaxed atmosphere, and good food. It is a perfect base from which to explore South Texas. You may find a weekend visit inadequate.

Reservations: (512) 943-1301. P.O. Box 4114, Port Isabel, Texas 78578. Doubles are $16 up, $25 for a two-room suite. Weekly rates for doubles is $100; $150 for two-room suites. Weekly rates are not available during summer.

Directions: Port Isabel is on the southernmost tip of Texas, twenty miles northeast of Brownsville. After arriving in Port Isabel on Texas Highway 100, turn left at Pancho's Kitchen, onto Yturria Street; The Yacht Club Hotel is two blocks off Highway 100.

## POINTS OF INTEREST

Port Isabel Lighthouse State Historic Site. Built in 1853, offers a fine view across Laguna Madre to South Padre Island. It is located near Texas 100, in Port Isabel.

Queen Isabella State Fishing Pier. More than a mile of abandoned highway causeway now used for fishing. Fish cleaning stations, fish attractor lights, restrooms, parking. On Texas 100, four miles east of Port Isabel on the south end of Padre Island.

Also see Points of Interest listed under La Posada in McAllen.

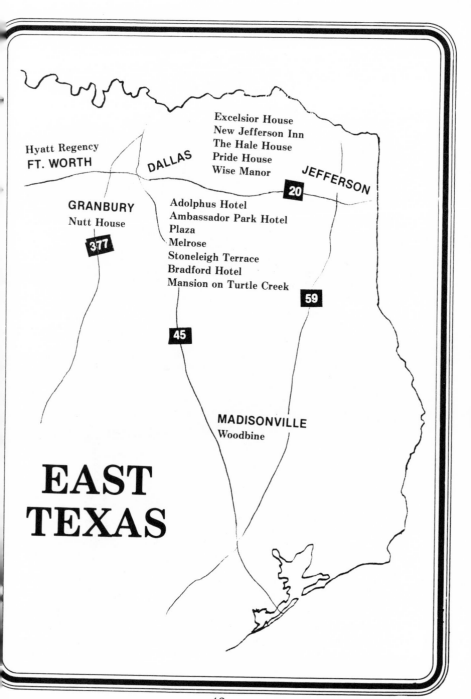

Hyatt Regency
**FT. WORTH**

**DALLAS**

Excelsior House
New Jefferson Inn
The Hale House
Pride House
Wise Manor

**JEFFERSON**

**20**

**GRANBURY**
Nutt House

**377**

Adolphus Hotel
Ambassador Park Hotel
Plaza
Melrose
Stoneleigh Terrace
Bradford Hotel
Mansion on Turtle Creek

**59**

**45**

**MADISONVILLE**
Woodbine

# EAST
# TEXAS

Excelsior House

# Excelsior House

*Jefferson*

Excelsior House is one of the most beautiful hotels in Texas. It's a surprise to find a hotel filled with the finest American antique furniture, French porcelain, crystal light fixtures, and Oriental rugs in a small town in East Texas. Its magnificent furnishings are all antiques and make the place a delight to discover piece by piece. When you leave at the end of your stay, you realize that you will probably not see another hotel as richly and exquisitely furnished as Excelsior House.

Built in the 1850s by Captain Perry, a New Hampshire sea captain, it was owned by several other individuals until 1961 when it was purchased by Jefferson's Jessie Allen Wise Garden Club. The members of the garden club have applied their considerable talent and love to the Excelsior's restoration. With the exception of the presence of television in the rooms, the Excelsior is perfectly furnished. The furniture (some bequeathed to the hotel by Jefferson residents), wallpaper patterns, light fixtures, and floor coverings have been carefully selected to convey a different theme in each room. The themes of the smaller rooms are more subtle than that of the grandly furnished show rooms: the music room's decorative pieces consist of only a piece of sheet music framed on the wall and a piano-shaped jewelry box on the table. The show rooms, rented last because of the daily tours, are particularly remarkable for their furniture or history. The Sleigh

Presidential Suite

Presidential Suite

Room contains a sleigh bed and dresser, which, along with the chest of drawers upstairs, is one of three complete sets of sleigh furniture in existence.

Lady Bird Johnson stays in the Lady Bird Johnson Room when she visits her nearby hometown of Karnack. The room contains some of the hotel's original rosewood furniture and a clock which was a wedding gift from Mrs. Johnson's father to her mother. A picture of Lyndon and Lady Bird is on the wall. Lady Bird's father's store and the house where she grew up can still be seen in nearby Karnack.

The Diamond Bessie room has a portrait of Diamond Bessie Moore and Abe Rothschild hanging on its wall. While staying at the Excelsior in 1877, Diamond Bessie was murdered. Bessie and Abe had left their room one Sunday for a picnic by the river; Bessie never returned, but Abe did, wearing Bessie's beautiful diamonds. Her body was discovered 10 days later. She had been shot and her expensive jewelry was gone. After seven years of sensational trials, Abe was acquitted, although public feeling ran very high against him. Some said that he paid each juror $1000 to find him not guilty. Bessie Moore's grave is in the Oakwood Cemetery in Jefferson.

Between the luxurious ballroom and the brickwalled courtyard is a small solarium where we ate a delicious breakfast of freshly-squeezed orange juice, coffee with real cream, ham, eggs, grits, bite-sized soda biscuits, and melt-in-your-mouth orange blossom muffins.

### Orange Blossom Muffins*

| | |
|---|---|
| 1 egg, slightly beaten | ½ c. orange marmalade |
| ¼ c. sugar | 2 c. biscuit mix |
| ½ c. orange juice | ½ c. chopped pecans |
| 2 T. oil or melted butter | |
| ¼ c. sugar | ¼ t. nutmeg |
| 1½ T. flour | 1 T. butter |
| ½ t. cinnamon | |

Mix ingredients. Sprinkle over batter in tins. Bake in 400°degree oven, 20-25 minutes.

*Recipe printed by permission of the Jessie Allen Wise Garden Club.

Mix ingredients. Sprinkle over batter in tins. Bake in 400 degree oven, 20-25 minutes.

Staying in Excelsior House is reason enough to visit Jefferson; however, the town is too interesting to ignore. Beginning in the 1850s, steamboats churned between Jefferson and New Orleans via the Big Cypress Bayou. Jefferson's population grew to 38,000 in the 1870s, making it the most populous city in Texas.

The steamboats had cabins so elegantly furnished that they surpassed the rooms of the finest hotels in the country. Each steamer had an Italian band which played at the landings, during meals, for balls in the evenings, or whenever passengers wanted to waltz or schottische. Jefferson had become "the Gateway to Texas" and the "Queen of the Cypress." This expansion was soon to end, however.

In 1873 Jay Gould came to town to seek right-of-way for his Texas Pacific Railway Company. Jefferson was loyal to the river traffic and refused his request. Angered by this rejection, Gould left his curse: "Jefferson will see the day when bats will roost in its church belfries and grass will grow in its streets". Still visible on the Excelsior's register is Jay Gould's signature and the words "End of Jefferson, Texas, Jan. 2, 1872".

The railroad was built around Jefferson and soon afterward the dam which made the Big Cypress navigable was blown up, ending this highly prosperous era for Jefferson. Some say that Jay Gould was instrumental in destroying the dam. Jefferson did shrink in size and economic importance but has retained its beauty and graciousness.

Jefferson claims several interesting firsts. It had the first artificial gas plant in Texas. It was the first city in Texas to produce artificial ice. Jefferson had the first brewery in Texas. It was the first steamboat metropolis in Texas. The first plows manufactured in Texas were designed and produced by Kelly Plow Company, an iron foundry in Kellyville, an early suburb of Jefferson.

The people who came to Jefferson built mansions similar to the homes they had left: French Colonial, Early American, Texas Colonial, and later, Victorian. All types are still in existence in Jefferson. Most have been restored and many are owned by descendants of the original owners. An historical pilgrimage, which tours many of these homes, is sponsored by the Jessie Allen Wise Garden Club each spring to commemorate the rich heritage of Jefferson.

Reservations: (214) 665-2513. 211 W. Austin St., Jefferson, Texas 75657. $20 up. $30 for Presidential Suite. Not all rooms have private baths.

Directions: Jefferson is on U.S. 59. Coming from the south to Jefferson, turn right on Highway 49 and follow signs to the Excelsior House. From Dallas, take I-20 to Marshall, then U.S. 59 north to Jefferson.

POINTS OF INTEREST

Jay Gould's private railroad car across the street from the hotel

Jefferson Historical Society Museum, next door to the hotel. Filled with antique farm tools, Caddo Indian relics, antique furniture and clothes, paintings.

Oakwood Cemetery

Historical buildings — 57 have the Texas Historical Marker

Antique shops

Big Cypress Bayou, steamboat rides on the *Cypress Queen*

Lake of the Pines, fishing, boating, swimming, good fried catfish at Lakeside Inn, 10 miles west of Jefferson

Caddo Lake

Marshall Pottery Company, Marshall, Texas. Famous for traditional Texas pottery

*Recipe printed by permission of the Jessie Allen Wise Garden Club.

New Jefferson Inn

# New Jefferson Inn

## Jefferson

In 1861, the New Jefferson Inn was built as a warehouse for storing bales of cotton. The walls were eight feet thick at the bottom of the foundation and tapered to 18 inches at its top. In 1900, with the demise of the river traffic, the building was converted to a hotel with a restaurant on the first floor. In the 1930s, WPA workers paved the street running in front of the hotel, and townspeople would bring box lunches to them. The dining room became a favorite place to go for dinner on a Sunday outing and remained so through the 1950s.

When Mr. and Mrs. George Delk of Dallas bought the hotel in 1977, it had become quite run down. They reopened it in April 1979, after putting in paneling, carpeting, new paint, air-conditioners, acoustical tile, showers, and whatever else that was necessary to make it clean and neat. Some of the original furniture was saved, and several of the original ceiling fans are still in use. Each room is different with its eclectic assortment of furniture pieces. The rooms feel more spacious than they are due to the 10-12 foot ceilings.

The restaurant is closed on Monday. It is open Tuesday—Sunday for breakfast and lunch, and Friday and Saturday for supper.

Reservations: (214) 665-2631, 124 West Austin Street, Jefferson, Tx 75657, $20 single, $22.50 double, $30 suite.

Directions: U.S. 59 N. Just before getting into Jefferson, take a right by the sign that says Jefferson Historical District. Follow signs to the Excelsior House. Or take a right on U.S. 49 off U.S. 59.

### POINTS OF INTEREST

See the Excelsior House

51

The Hale House

# The Hale House

## Jefferson

The Hale House is the private home of Katharine Galloway, which she purchased in 1978 and opened for overnight guests on April 17, 1981, in time for Jefferson's annual historic Pilgrimage. Accommodations are upstairs in a separate part of the house, with its own covered entrance way on the side. There are two large rooms which have been pleasantly decorated with antique beds enlarged to queen size, old writing tables, and several other pieces of furniture on polished wood floors. The shared bathroom is equally inviting with its footed tub, wood table, and sunny windows. In the hallway between the two rooms is an appliance for coffee or tea. Kate rents the two rooms as a unit to one person or a group as large as four.

The main part of the house was built in 1865 in the Greek Revival style. There were four rooms and a central hall, typical of houses on the street. The Greek Revival style had been popular in the East 20 years before and then swept westward. It was probably built by a local carpenter for a steamboat captain or someone connected with the river, since river related jobs were in abundance at that time, and the people put up simple homes to meet their needs.

May Belle Hale came to this house with her family at two years of age in 1882. May Belle became a prominent Jefferson civic leader who taught music, and at one time she had three symphony orchestras. In the 1920s, she

Built in 1865 in Greek revival style

enlarged her home to its present size and turned it into a boarding house. If you look at the side of the house, you can see the original structure with its wide siding and the addition with its narrow boards. She reportedly served delicious meals. During the Depression the Hale House was lively with May Belle's music and civic activities, boarders, and dances. Dance groups unable to find work were glad to perform at May Belle's for the responsive townspeople.

Reservations: (214) 665-8555, Box 10, Jefferson, Tx 75657 $35.

Directions: Get instructions from K. Galloway.

POINTS OF INTEREST

See the Excelsior House

# The Pride House

*Jefferson*

On our first trip to Jefferson, we had stopped at a handsome structure, arresting in its photographic appeal. Vacant, with peeling paint, cobwebs, and overgrown shrubs, it made us wonder what its past had been. What a surprise after making arrangements by telephone for a hotel in Jefferson called the Pride House, to find out it was the same place photographed earlier, now striking in its beauty. Ray and Sandy Spalding fell in love with the house and bought it in September 1979. It had been vacant since 1969, when a fire had seriously damaged the house. The Bender family had lived in it for 47 years, since 1922, but they decided the damage was too extensive for them to repair.

The house, sometimes known as the Gingerbread House by the townspeople, was built by George W. Brown in 1889. Brown owned a lumbermill, and the work was supervised by his father-in-law, Captain Welch. The materials and workmanship are superb. The studs are 2x6 and go through from the bottom of the house to the roof. There are three layers of wood on the outside: the siding, the sheeting, and another sheeting.

The house has lovely beaded wainscoting, 12-foot ceilings, and long windows which make sunny, attractive bedrooms. Look at the ornately carved door knobs, hinges, and window latches. The windows are a special attraction. The top half of each window is surrounded by squares of different colors of stained glass. The exterior

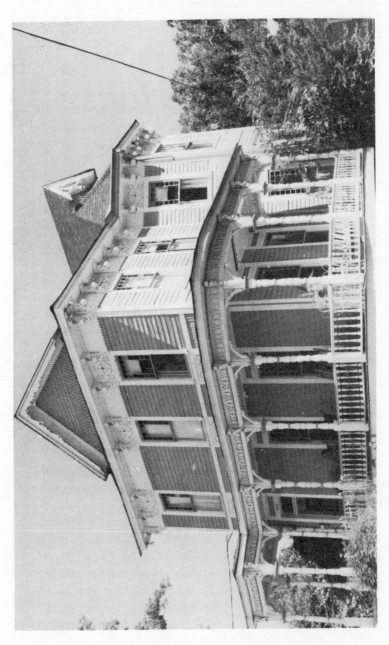

The Pride House

has been painted a caramel tan with cream trim, and there are touches of blue everywhere. This color scheme is carried through the house also. There are caramel carpets everywhere except the parlor, caramel walls, and an interesting colorful paper cutout trim edging the ceiling in the hallways.

Ray and Sandy have moved on but left behind Sandy's mother, Ruthmary, as innkeeper. Visitors are in luck. It is evident that she loves to meet people and is a hospitable and gracious host. She plans to make a few changes, such as possibly including meals in her dining room, but there is no doubt the changes will be met with approval.

There are numerous trees and shrubs around the house, such as wisteria, pecans, catalpa, and Kadota figs. Guests are welcome to pick and eat the fruit, and in fig season, you will probably be served preserves made from the figs .

The Pride House is a bed and breakfast place. Until Ruthmary revises the breakfast location, breakfast will be waiting in an armoire in the upstairs hall. At our visit there was orange juice, coffee, tea, strawberries, bananas, cream, and whole wheat raisin muffins. There were trays and beautiful English cups and plates decorated with strawberries to take into your room or out onto the wide front porch.

Each room is different in layout, decor, and atmosphere, but all have ceiling fans, central air and heat, firm mattresses, portable TV's upon request, and private phones. Large armoires provide closet space. The shower heads contain Shaklee's liquid cleaner, Basic-H, which is released as suds when the lever is switched. One of the rooms has a fireplace, and Sandy and Ruthmary had fun in the winter lighting the fire, then watching the delighted faces of unsuspecting guests as they entered the room for the first time.

The key you are given is to the front door, not your room. The Spaldings couldn't bear the thought of defac-

Parlor                    Pride Houst 1978

Dependency

ing the beautifully carved door knobs and hardware to install room locks. An antique bassinet is available for babies, and it might be possible to get a baby sitter if arranged in advance.

Families with children usually stay in the Dependency. A dependency is any outbuilding where people live which relies on the main house. In this case, the dependency was originally for servants. It is a regular two-story house with two bedrooms and a kitchen where breakfast makings are provided. It can accommodate six guests.

If you wish to partake of the Excelsior's famous breakfast, the Pride House will make reservations for you.

Oh, yes. It is called the Pride House after the Spalding's small son, Pride. They wanted to name it the Gingerbread House, but the name had already been taken.

Reservations: (214) 665-2675, 409 Broadway, Jefferson, Tx 75657, $40, two people, $5 each additional person. No pets. Closed during Pilgrimage, first weekend in May.

Directions: U.S. 59 N. Just before getting into Jefferson, take a right by the sign that says Jefferson Historical District. Take a left at the first traffic light. Or take a right on US. S 49 off U.S. 59.

POINTS OF INTEREST

See the Excelsior House

Wise Manor

# Wise Manor

*Jefferson*

The Wise Manor was built in 1851 by Captain Moorings from Mooringsport, Louisiana, as a two-room structure. The house has been in Katherine Wise's family since 1866. An aunt owned it from 1874 until 1928, when Katherine moved there. It is now a one and one-half-story gingerbread cottage, having been enlarged to its present size in 1874. The only other changes were made by Katherine's side of the family in the late '20s.

Here is your chance to stay in a house that is on the walking tour of Jefferson's historic homes. It is in a quiet residential area a few blocks off a main street. When you look out the front door, you will see a field of wild flowers. The rooms are upstairs, and you will be given a key to the front door. There is no air-conditioning, but Mrs. Wise says the house stays delightfully cool in the summer. There are two rooms, each with its own bathroom. One room has a double bed, and the two connecting rooms have both a single and a double bed. Coffee is available in the morning.

Staying at the Wise Manor will be like staying at a relative's house. Members of the same family have lived in it for over 100 years, so it is furnished with the family pieces. The guest rooms have not been cleared out and redecorated for overnight guests, but have been left as they probably were when vacated by the last child to leave home. The rooms are cozy and inviting. One bed has a family quilt which is over 100 years old. Against the wall is a primitive pine box and an old handmade shawl draped over it.

One of the most interesting aspects of the accommodations is the beds. The youth bed was handmade of walnut in 1885 and is extra long. Katharine found the handmade pine double bed in a farm house corncrib. She paid $20 for the bed and a trip to the hospital for the resulting allergy attack. She is almost certain the other double bed is a Malard bed from Louisiana, with its huge headboard and Malard's signature egg in the center top of the elaborate carving.

Reservations: (214) 665-2386 - home, (214) 665-7161 - office. 312 Houston, Jefferson, Tx 75657. $35 one room, $40 connecting rooms, $50 both units.

Directions: U.S. 59 North. Just before getting into Jefferson, take a right by the sign that says Jefferson Historical District. Take a left at the first traffic light. Or take a right on U.S. 49 off U.S. 59. Take a right on Line St. After 8 or 9 blocks, take a left on Houston.

POINTS OF INTEREST

See the Excelsior House

# Adolphus Hotel

## Dallas

The Adolphus Hotel building is truly magnificent. Ornate plaster carvings line the doors and lower-level windows. The base is red granite, and the walls are of Oriental tapestry brick and gray granite. Under a roof of variegated slate and antique green bronze are sculptured figures representing night and morning, Apollo, Mercury, Ceres, gargoyles, and heraldic characters of many kinds. The figures can be seen from the ground at Commerce or Akard Street.

Adolphus Busch, founder of the Anheuser Busch Breweries, created this luxurious hotel. Adolphus owned a brewery supply business in St. Louis when he married Lilly Anheuser in 1861. After the Civil War, he sold the supply business and went to work for his father-in-law as a salesman for the struggling Anheuser Brewery. Adolphus wanted to expand the beer's distribution. He wanted to ship beer all over the U.S., not just to Missouri, and he wanted to ship it in freight cars refrigerated with ice. His test state was Texas, and the beer was a great success.

Adolphus Busch developed an attachment to the state that helped make him successful. In 1910 he decided that the growth of Dallas would support a fine hotel which he wanted to be as palatial as the Blackstone in Chicago. Adolphus gathered together leading citizens of Dallas and told them that if they would buy a small number of shares in this hotel, he would finance the rest.

Adolphus Hotel

They agreed and bought 10 percent of the shares. The hotel was completed in 1912. It cost $1,800,000 and was the tallest building in Texas.

When Adolphus died in 1913, the Busch family continued to operate the hotel. The 3000 square foot Skyway Suite was the Dallas home of the Busch family. The Century Room opened in the late '30s as a dinner club featuring such entertainers as Phil Harris and Liberace. It had a rink for ice shows, a retractable wood floor for dancing, and two-story windows. In 1949 they sold it to Leo Corrigan, Sr. His son was the next owner until 1980, when it was sold to Westgroup, Inc. of Los Angeles, and New England Life Insurance Company.

The new owners spent 18 months and $45 million to return it to its gilded rococo splendor. The most dramatic change has been in the rooms. There had been more than 800 ordinary, small rooms, but there are now 437 beautifully decorated huge rooms. Room furnishings are custom-made Chippendale and Queen Anne style furniture, with Axminster carpeting from England. There is a work or dining table, desk, separate sitting area with sofa, occasional chairs, and a coffee table. Live plants and prints provide decoration. In the bathroom are terrycloth bathrobes, three kinds of soap, shampoo, cream rinse, shoe polish, and a telephone. Each room is soundproof.

The stairwells have been pressurized against smoke, and all rooms and halls have smoke alarms, sprinklers, and a public address system for communicating fire escape and emergency procedures.

The Adolphus also has 15 suites, some with outdoor terraces and roof-top skylights, 11 private meeting rooms, a palatial grand ballroom and Louis XV-style several bars. The grand ballroom and Louis XV-style French Room restaurant are magnificent. The walls and vaulted ceilings are adorned with ornate, 18th century murals and edged with gilt. Enormous glass chandeliers have been specially hand blown in the pastel pink and

Adolphus Hotel

green colors of the murals and the 59-hued carpeting custom made in Hong Kong.

A drive-in entrance with street-level registration has been added at one end of the lobby, but the main lobby has not changed much from before the restoration, since it was still very handsome with its oil paintings, marble chests, and beautiful paneling of magnolia and black walnut. However, a large percentage of the restoration costs have been spent to add rare tapestries, lamps, furniture, clocks, paintings, and carpeting to the lobby area. There is a six-foot, 19th-century French portrait of Napolean Bonaparte; Brussels' tapestries made in 1661; Oriental, American, and European pieces; and carpeting made in England or Hong Kong.

A favorite Adolphus treasure is the gilt chandelier between the main lobby and the registration desk. It is one of a pair commissioned by Adolphus Busch for the Anheuser Busch exhibit at the 1904 St. Louis World's Fair. This circular chandelier is made of small lights representing hops berries scattered among gilt leaves of the hop plant. After the exposition, both chandeliers hung for several years in the company's Clydesdale horse barn. One then went to the St. Louis Museum and the other to the Adolphus Hotel.

It is worth a trip to the Adolphus even if only to look at the exquisite furnishings.

Reservations: (214) 747-6411, 1321 Commerce, Dallas, Tx 75221, Rates are $85-$125 for singles, $100-$140 for doubles, and $200-$500 for suites.

Directions: The Adolphus Hotel is in downtown Dallas on Commerce and Akard Sts.

POINTS OF INTEREST

See the Stoneleigh Terrace.

Ambassador Park Hotel

# Ambassador Park Hotel

## Dallas

Restoration of the oldest hotel in Dallas, the Ambassador Park Hotel, should be complete in the spring of
1982, and it promises to make the Ambassador a landmark once again. The exact beginnings of the Ambassador are uncertain, but it appears that the hotel was
built in 1905 as the Majestic (an appropriate name for
this building) across from City Park and Browder
Springs. The Majestic was Dallas' first suburban luxury
hotel and the first high-rise residential hotel west of the
Mississippi River.

The adjoining City Park was Dallas' first public
park. Browder Springs, located in the park, had been
developed into a private waterworks, which the city
bought in 1869, and for many years was the city's only
source of water. When the 10 acres of land were being
considered for purchase, there was a big hubbub over
whether the city should spend $600 so frivolously. The
park later brought the intersection of two major
railroads to Dallas when a bill was passed requiring the
routes to intersect within one mile of Browder Springs.

The hotel was sold to Frederick W. Boedeker in
1908. Boedeker was born in Westphalia, Germany, and
had come to Dallas in 1886, where he had set up a confec-
tionary business. By the time he purchased the Majestic,
he was president of his ice and ice cream company,

Boedeker Manufacturing Company. He made extensive changes in the hotel, putting in a new heating system, side porch, awnings, and changing the name to the Park, due to its proximity to City Park. At that time, the area around the hotel was called the Cedars, an area of wealthy Jewish people. In fact, the hotel served only kosher food for quite some time.

With its spacious rooms, high ceilings, wide hallways, and gas lights, the hotel was an elegant, aristocratic setting for debutante balls and socials. It was the first hotel west of the Mississippi to have elevators. In 1932, its name was changed to the Ambassador, additions were made to the building, and modern plumbing and a sprinkler system were installed. Eventually the hotel became a nursing home, then was in estate for seven years. In 1955, Col. C.R. Tips, a member of the Dallas City Historical Survey Committee, bought the hotel and converted it into Dallas' first retirement residence. At the present time, it is a mixture of old and young people.

When restoration is complete this spring, the hotel will be a personal service hotel for people who plan to be in Dallas several days to a week or longer. It is being modeled after the Windsor Arms in Toronto, by Sadru Alini, whose family has been in the hotel business for over 200 years. Most of the credit for the new life of the hotel belongs to Gene Riggs, the project manager and general manager, who lives in the hotel. Gene had known of the Ambassador for years, and about five years before, had attended a party in one of the hotel's penthouse apartments. When it came up for sale, Sadru, for whom Gene had done a lot of contract work, said he would purchase it if Gene would oversee the project and run the hotel. Gene didn't have to think long about such an opportunity, so in February, 1981, Sadru bought the place and Gene moved in.

As work started, it was soon evident that the old building would be a worker's dream. It was built solidly and well, with good materials. The construction is of brick and stucco, with some steel. The pipe is copper. The oak structural beams are 8x8, with a burn time of seven hours, twice as long as most buildings. Riggs said it has the best sprinkler system in town. The new carpets, bedspreads, draperies, and upholstery have been chosen with patterns and colors which were popular at the turn of the century. Predominant colors are maroon, green, and peach.

There will be a full service restaurant specializing in American cuisine, a refreshing attitude to those tired of hearing European atmosphere and French food touted as being the most desirable. A good old American hotel with American food. It will be interesting to see the menu. There will be three meeting rooms which can open to a large ballroom for 300. The Ambassador plans to have shuttle service to the airport, market, convention center, and shopping. There are 130 rooms now, but upon completion, there will be 110, and each room should have an excellent view, particularly the ones on the side of City Park and the freeway interchanges.

Trees surrounding the hotel give the feeling of a quiet residential area, even though it is right on the edge of downtown. If the work is done as planned, the Ambassador Park Hotel should once again be full of life, lovely, gracious, and a desirable gathering place.

Reservations: (214) 565-9003 $85 double.

Directions: The Ambassador Park Hotel is on the south of downtown Dallas where Ervay and St. Paul meet.

POINTS OF INTEREST

See the Stoneleigh Terrace.

The Plaza

72

# The Plaza

*Dallas*

In 1923, with six hotels already in his possession, Conrad N. Hilton realized that Texas had expensive hotels and dumps, but nothing in between. He found a suitable lot and sketched a 15-story hotel for the average traveler. The construction estimates of one million dollars slowed him a bit, until he realized he wanted to do it so much that he would somehow have to create some financing plans. The first thing he did was answer an ad in a New York newspaper appealing to those with financing problems. He returned from New York with no hotel construction money but with a $100,000 insurance policy. He eventually found financing for the hotel, but not without difficulty.

August 4, 1925, the steel, concrete, and brick hotel trimmed with terra cotta and stone opened with Jack White as general manager. They took out full page ads in the newspapers.

|            |      |
|------------|------|
| 48 rooms   | 1.50 |
| 48 rooms   | 1.75 |
| 24 rooms   | 2.00 |
| 120 rooms  | 2.50 |
| 80 rooms   | 3.00 |

... and think of the rates in a beautiful, absolutely fireproof hotel, furnished to "a Queen's taste" with every modern convenience

Remodeled Interior

including such equipment as Sealy Inner Spring Mattresses and Box Springs, Simmons Beds, Bigelow—Hartford Carpets and *Not One West Room.*

The elevators, laundry chute, and air shafts had been put on the west side of the building, insulating the 325 rooms from the afternoon sun. Hilton had created a slogan for the new hotel which he registered and used for the next 25 years: "Minimax-Minimum Charge for Maximum Service." The Dallas-Hilton was a success from its opening day. Jack White eventually became the owner and changed its name to White Plaza.

The current history of the Plaza revolves around a dynamic woman, Opal Sebastian. In 1977, she was selling real estate and looking for a hotel building for a client. The Plaza was for sale in bankruptcy and in terrible shape, but Opal thought it was so attractive that the client would grab it immediately. He hated it, but by then, the hotel was in her blood. On November 15, 1977, she became the Plaza's new owner. Up went the shirt sleeves, out went linoleum, shoe shine stands, carpets, vagrants, grime, and on went new paint. There were no pillows, blankets, or sheets. As the money came in, improvements were made, beginning with paint, then carpet and new drapes, and the floors were reopened one by one.

By May 1980 there was enough money to redo the lobby. The abundant mahogany paneling and 20-foot white ceilings with molded plaster were retained. Dracenas in brass planters came from the Adolphus Hotel and are tall enough to resemble palms. Brass and glass chandeliers send sparkles of light everywhere. The atmosphere is slightly elegant, yet cozy and warm.

The round brass wall plaque over one entrance was found in the basement storage, as was an enormous round brass planter. A beautiful brass letter box by the elevators gleams again. Off to one side of the lobby is the comfortable bar, Sebastian's. Its beautiful back bar was imported to a California hotel from England 100 years ago, and about 10 years ago, found its way to the Plaza.

One of the most interesting aspects of the rooms is the dramatic wallpaper in many styles. If you can't live with the choice in your room, ask to see another, because there is bound to be one to suit you. The ceilings in the rooms are nine feet, except for a few which have been lowered. The windows are large and operable. The bathrooms are spick and span and have a slightly 1920s feel to them. The 240 rooms include 17 suites and three apartments. The Plaza is reminiscent of some of the Paris hotels, and in fact has many foreign visitors. There is a concierge available, and there are employees who speak Arabic, Spanish, French, and Chinese.

There are armed guard patrolling the building. This is comforting to anyone in a downtown hotel and especially to women travelling alone. The outside fire escape has been painted to blend in with the exterior and is in good working order.

The Plaza continues Hilton's "Minimax" tradition since the rooms are very reasonable for a hotel in the downtown of a major city. Ms. Sebastian has sought the business of the increasing number of foreign travelers, women travelers, business people who are paying for their own expenses, families on vacations, and groups traveling who wish to stay together and as cheaply as possible.

Reservations: Dallas (214) 742-7251, Texas, 800-442-7271, Continental U.S.A.—800-527-9374, 1933 Main St., Dallas, Tx 75201. $35—single, $45-double, $48-twin, $75-$200—suite.

Directions: The Plaza is in the east side of downtown Dallas at Main and Harwood.

### POINTS OF INTEREST
See the Stoneleigh Terrace

# Melrose Hotel

## Dallas

Although the name has not changed, the classic 1924 Melrose Hotel will introduce a new face at opening in late December, 1982.

The highly detailed columns, panelling and wood work of the public areas have been restored and enhanced. The natural light from the windows creates a brillant reflection on the elegant dark green marble flooring of the lobby area. Creating a warm glow in the evening hours, are two custom seven-foot diameter brass and glass chandeliers, one positioned directly over the center grouping. The original entrance to the hotel will be closed to provide a private courtyard to be used for afternoon cocktails, private dining and receptions. Guest rooms will be furnished with lush oriental rugs and renners and beautiful period furniture.

The Melrose was designed and built in 1924 by C.D. Hill, who moved to Dallas and established the architectural firm of C.D. Hill and Co. The land on which the hotel is situated was originally the site of a home built in 1889 by Colonel George Mellersh, a Civil War veteran. At that time the surrounding area was open farm land. In 1904, the property was purchased and the house renovated by Ballard M. Burgher, a prominent banker and real estate investor. After completion, the Melrose was known for its old world charm and its atmosphere of comfort and hospitality. Each of its guest rooms had an outside exposure and 100 of the guest rooms had kitchen facilities. In more recent years, the hotel housed many

Melrose Hotel

permanent residents and frequently was used as a residence for musicians and touring companies.

The eight-story hotel will have 185 guest rooms and suites, a 125-seat restaurant, an 85-seat lounge and approximately 5,000 square feet of meeting facilities.

Directions: The Melrose is located two miles northwest of downtown Dallas.

Reservations: Call (214) 521-5151, 3015 Oak Lawn Avenue, Dallas, Texas 75219. Rates will be in the $80 to $150 range.

POINTS OF INTEREST

See Points of Interest for the Stoneleigh Terrace.

The Library Restaurant

Stoneleigh Terrace

# Stoneleigh Terrace

*Dallas*

Staying at the Stoneleigh Terrace has become a tradition for show business people who visit Dallas. Perhaps it is popular with entertainers because it is such a quiet restful place away from crowds, a contrast to their profession. Or perhaps it is because the Stoneleigh Terrace is so artistically furnished. The lobby is as welcoming as the canopied walkway and friendly stone lions at the front entrance. It has sunny, full-length windows on the outside wall, nicely coordinated furnishings in pleasing shades of blues and golds, fresh flowers, and several large oil paintings. The hall of the floor we were on had peach and white striped wall paper and peach-colored lamps beside each doorway.

The Stoneleigh Terrace was built in 1926 and has retained its charm throughout the years. It is managed by Inter City Investments and has 154 rooms. The rooms vary a good deal, both in layout, decor, general atmosphere, and type of accommodation. They are decorated in a great variety of fabrics, light fixtures, and furniture styles, all very pleasing and comfortable. All the rooms are larger than the rooms of new hotels, with space for a sofa and chairs or a writing table. Many rooms have a small dressing room with a large mirror and good lighting, and there are new thick carpets and fresh paint. The large wood frame windows still open and close. The only complaint we had was the thin walls.

Efficiency apartments and larger apartments are

Colorful entrance

Apartments available

also available which would be good choices for families traveling with several children or for anyone wanting a kitchen. Apartment seekers may consider leasing the 7,000 square foot penthouse created in 1937 and 1938 out of space occupied by kitchens, dining rooms, and a ballroom.

The hotel services include the use of a van and driver for transportation, room service, and free parking. The apartment building in the next block has a swimming pool, tennis courts, and a washateria which hotel guests are invited to use. Hotel service people are available, but scarce, so you're basically on your own, which is sometimes very nice.

The Stoneleigh Terrace is only two miles from downtown Dallas and is on a bus line, making the downtown area accessible. The hotel is within walking distance (three to six blocks) of many antique and art shops and several excellent restaurants.

Reservations: (214) 742-7111. 2927 Maple Avenue, Dallas, Texas 75222. Doubles are $40 up.

Directions: The Stoneleigh Terrace is two miles northwest of downtown Dallas on Maple Avenue.

## POINTS OF INTEREST

Many good restaurants within walking distance of the Stoneleigh Terrace.

State Fair Park. 200-acre home of nation's largest annual state fair. Held for 16 days during October. Permanent exhibits are on display during the remainder of the year.

John F. Kennedy Memorials. Cenotaph and Memorial Park at Main and Market Streets downtown. John F. Kennedy Museum at 501 Elm Street.

Lakes. Many nearby lakes for fishing, swimming

and boating: Bachman, Grapevine, Lavon, Lewisville, Mountain Creek, Ray Hubbard, White Rock.

Texas Stadium Tour. Tour of Dallas Cowboys' stadium.

Shopping. Shopping is a pleasant part of a trip to Dallas since the city is a major center for clothes and all types of imports. Some interesting shopping centers are these: Olla Podrida (12215 Coit Road) for arts and crafts, Sanger Harris stores (the downtown store is at 303 N. Akard), Old Town Village (5500 Greenville Avenue) for imports, and The Quadrangle (2800 Routh) for specialty shops.

Six Flags Over Texas. Huge entertainment park, its six sections devoted to Texas' colorful past under the flags of Spain, France, Mexico, the Republic, the Confederacy and the United States. Consists of rides including Shock Wave, the world's longest, tallest, and fastest double-loop roller coaster, pirate island, frontier gunfights, Indian ceremonies, refreshments, and staged entertainment. Open daily during the summer. On Dallas-Ft. Worth Turnpike midway between the two cities.

International Wildlife Park. 5.4-mile motor trail through wild animal park. Free-roaming animals include hippos, rhinos, camels, antelope, zebras, waterfowl, and giraffes. The park is situated off the Dallas-Ft. Worth Turnpike (I-30) at Belt Line Road in the city of Grand Prairie. Phone (214) 263-2201 for additional information.

City Park. South side of downtown.

# The Bradford Hotel

## Dallas

By 1925 the economy of Dallas was booming. Business was so brisk, in fact, that the city had 7,500 hotel rooms. Even this was insufficient, as the development of the Plaza (1925) and the Stoneleigh Terrace (1926) can attest. In addition, on October 5, 1925, the Scott Hotel opened across from the train station in time for the State Fair. It was built by George C. Scott, financed by Genara Realty, designed by Land and Witchell, and built by Jopling-Marshall Construction.

The grand opening had music by the Jack Gardner orchestra and was broadcast live on Station WFAA. The opening day advertisement read:

The Scott Hotel
Modern — Fireproof — Comfortable
A Ceiling Fan in Every Room
Every Bed a Sealy
160 Rooms — 160 Baths
Rates $2.00 and $2.50

The hotel was constructed of fireproof brick, reinforced concrete, and carved terra cotta trim. There was a drugstore on the first floor and barber shop and toilet facilities in the basement. Two elevators (advertised as high speed) took guests up to the 10 floors of the building. It was a first class hotel.

The hotel was remodeled in 1948, when mahogany furniture and ceiling fans were replaced with modern furniture and air conditioning, and the name was changed

The Dallas Bradford

to the Lawrence Hotel. A second remodeling took place in 1952, but by the 1960s, the hotel had deteriorated. In 1980, the Kerr Company of Minneapolis came to the rescue, and it is a beautiful first class hotel again. Extensive remodeling was done, leaving only the basic room structure, the bathrooms, and the lobby's molded plaster ceiling trim. The name was changed to the Bradford Hotel, after the Dailsy Bradford, the first oil well in Texas. There are now 132 rooms. An excellent job of combining old with new has been achieved. For example, some might have considered detrimental the bright turquoise, orange, pink, or green bathroom tile. But instead of disguising or removing it, the Bradford has made the color the focal point of the room, being shown to best advantage by the subdued grays, browns, and tans, of the bedrooms. It is an excellent way of handling a decorating problem and causes the outdated colors to be seen in a new light.

Another outstanding decorating aspect is the color scheme. Burgundy, gray, and tan are the dominant colors. The lobby has accents of green in a wide lime stripe in the carpet, the enormous spathyphlum and palms, and the huge leaf murals. The china in the restaurant reflects the burgundy of the main carpet and the gold of the brass which is found throughout the hotel. Bamboo is another unifying item, both in its color and use.

The rooms are standard 12' x 12' size of the commercial hotels built between 1912 and 1945, but the Bradford turns their size into an asset by describing the rooms as cozy and charming, which they definitely are. There is track lighting and handsome brass lamps. The beds are queen size with comfortable firm mattresses. Each room has an excellent view of the many tourist attractions which are within easy walking distance. The bus is close by, and the hotel also has free parking.

The Bradford Hotel is a pleasant place to stay. The staff is friendly and professional. The hotel has a

*Courtesy of the Bradford House*

restaurant which serves delicious food and a bar, The Brass Hippo, which displays a wonderful brass hippopotamus.

Reservations: (800) 442-7292 (Tx), (800) 527-9265 (rest of U.S.), (214) 761-9090 (Dallas). Jackson at Houston St., Dallas, Texas 75202. $75 and up. Ask for corporate rates.

Directions: The Bradford House is in downtown Dallas across from Union Station and Reunion Arena. Look for the ball on the top of the Reunion Tower.

POINTS OF INTEREST

See the Stoneleigh Terrace.

# Mansion on Turtle Creek

## Dallas

The Mansion on Turtle Creek contains antique Chinese ceramics, fresh flowers, 18th-century French tapestries, fine furniture, marble, and brass statuary. Not many places supply Kleenex boxes made of abalone shell or give guests a whole box of chocolates instead of the one bedside chocolate. The employees are friendly and anxious to serve and please each guest.

The service and beauty of the hotel are not the only items of interest. The Mansion is another hotel which has utilized an historical structure on its grounds in a way that brings the building back to life and fulfills a vital function for the hotel. In this case, an old home has been converted into the hotel's restaurant.

In the early 1900s the Armstrong family began developing what they hoped would become the city's most exclusive residential area, to be called Highland Park. Sheppard W. King, Jr. built the third mansion in this development, which was completed in 1908.

The Kings, who had made their fortune in cotton, had their home demolished in 1923 after deciding they wanted a fancier place. Mr. and Mrs. King and their architect, J. Allen Boyle, left for Europe to spend two years collecting ideas for their new home. They wrote their building contractor constantly so that he could keep the plans updated. Their new home was completed in 1925. It was built in 16th-century Italian style with a touch of Spain evident in the stucco archways and wrought iron trim.

Mansion on Turtle Creek

Typical suite
*Courtesy of The Mansion on Turtle Creek*

Mansion on Turtle Creek Restaurant
*Courtesy of the Mansion on Turtle Creek*

91

Architectural elements collected during the Kings' tour, such as the carved woodwork and marble columns, were incorporated into the design. Most of the home's features are still in evidence.

In 1935, the Kings sold the Mansion to Freeman Burford and his wife Carolyn Skelly. The original architect was retained to update the house. In the late 1940s the Mansion was converted into offices. It served various businesses until bought by Rosewood Hotels, Inc. (owned by the Hunt family) in 1979. The building was restored and then opened for business as a restaurant in August, 1980.

The main dining area was once the salon of the residence. Its ceiling is made of 2400 pieces of enameled and inlaid wood which required six craftsmen two months to install. The bedrooms have been converted to private dining rooms, and the original dining room and kitchen have been converted to a lounge and bar. The restaurant is managed by the famed 21 Company of New York. A nine-story, 175-room hotel was added to the grounds in a matching architectural style, opening in April of 1981.

The Mansion on Turtle Creek would be a good choice for a special occasion.

Reservations: (800) 527-5432 (outside Texas) or (800) 442-3408 (in Texas). Restaurant number is (214) 526-2121. 2821 Turtle Creek Boulevard, Dallas, Texas 75219. $160 for a double room, $400 and up for a suite.

Directions: The Mansion is located on Turtle Creek, off Hall Street, approximately two miles north of downtown Dallas.

## POINTS OF INTEREST
See Stoneleigh Terrace listing.

# Hyatt Regency Fort Worth

*Fort Worth*

This hotel is another big city hotel built when people realized their city had everything but a fancy place to meet socially or for business. Fort Worth, named after General William Jenkins Worth, had seen steady growth since its beginnings as a frontier army post in 1849. It became a gateway to both the West for travelers, and to the North for the Chisholm Trail cattle drives. Fort Worth became an important center for the cattle industry, and in 1917, oil was struck at Ranger, Texas, 80 miles west of Fort Worth. Thus, in 1919, some Fort Worth business leaders sat down to figure out financing possibilities for a hotel to match the growing importance of this city "where the West begins".

This investment group, calling themselves the Citizens Hotel Company, raised $1.2 million among themselves, then sought outside investors. Within a few months they were able to raise an additional $1.8 million from nearly 800 Fort Worth citizens. Construction on the new hotel, to be the tallest high-rise in town, began in 1920.

The first name considered for the hotel was the Winfield, in honor of Winfield Scott, a cattleman, builder, and banker who had contributed heavily to Fort Worth's development before his death in 1911. But they decided the hotel should be a part of Texas, not just Fort Worth,

Fort Worth Hyatt Regency

so it was named the Hotel Texas. The Hotel Texas opened on September 20, 1921. The grand opening was the main event of the day. All local newspaper ads asked, "What will *you* wear to the opening of the Hotel Texas?"

The Hotel Texas quickly became a focal point for the city and was nicknamed the Home of the Cattle Barons. Since that time famous guests have come and gone, one of the most famous being John F. Kennedy, who spent his last night at the Hotel Texas on November 21, 1963, before his fateful trip to Dallas. The Will Rogers Suite had been decorated for the President's visit, but Secret Service officers chose a smaller room with only one door for Kennedy so they could better protect him.

Hotel operators have also come and gone from the Hotel Texas, one of the more recent being the Sheraton Corporation. In 1978 the Woodbine Corporation, a subsidiary of Hunt Oil Company, bought the Hotel Texas from Sheraton to be managed by Hyatt Hotels Corporation. The Woodbine Corporation spent $35 million renovating the hotel. Since the insides of the hotel needed to be gutted due to its run-down condition, they discussed in what way it should be renovated. Should it look as it once did or should it be entirely modern in feeling, which would perhaps produce a nice contrast with the building's older exterior? They opted for the latter. So don't expect rooms filled with antiques or a lobby furnished with heavy wood furniture, rawhide and rope. Instead, be ready for a thoroughly modern old hotel: tiny blinking lights on floors, walls and ceilings; waterfalls and indoor plants. The magnificent tall arched windows of the lobby are partially blocked by a walkway set up with bar tables. The renovation of the old Texas Hotel does not bring back the 19th century, but it does mean the hotel is coming on strong and won't have to face the wrecking ball.

Reservations: (817) 870-1234. 815 Main Street, Fort Worth, Texas 76102. $65 and up for a double. Large suites available including a particularly nice Presidential Suite ($650)

Directions: The Hyatt Regency is in downtown Fort Worth next to the Convention Center.

## POINTS OF INTEREST

Amon G. Carter Museum of Western Art — Permanent collection of the paintings and sculpture of Frederick Remington and Charles Russell.

Casa Mañana Theater — Geodesic dome over notable theatre-in-the-round.

Kimbell Art Museum — 18th-century portraits and old masters in one of the world's finest museum buildings.

Lakes for boating, swimming, fishing.

Six Flags Over Texas Amusement Park — in nearby Arlington.

Stockyard Arena — Renovated Western-style stores and restaurants along Exchange Avenue on city's North Side.

# The Nutt House

## Granbury

The Nutt House is a delightful place to stay. It might be the same without owner Mary Lou Watkins there to run it, but it is doubtful. The presence of this charming woman is felt everywhere in the hotel and in the town of Granbury. On April 1, 1970, when Mary Lou completed restoration and began serving meals in her grandfather's store and hotel, it was surrounded by crumbling neglected buildings. Partially through her efforts and example, the entire square today is in the National Register of Historic Places and is a vital, interesting place to visit. In 1980 she opened the hotel rooms to overnight guests again, and word has quickly spread of the treat awaiting the traveler.

There are three singles, four doubles, and one suite, all sparsely but well decorated, as befits the drummers' rooms that they were. Each room has a sink, and there is a bathroom in each hall to be shared by the rooms on that side. The ceilings are 14 feet high, and there are 10-foot arched windows. The furnishings are antique beds, dressers, and a rattan mirror and shelf, rattan being a status symbol at the turn of the century. At the head of the stairs are wicker chairs, reading lamps, and enormous old chattel mortgage ledgers and receipt books from the late 1800s. The books are fun to look through, deciphering the ornate writing and chuckling at chattel of "one flea-bitten old mare".

The hotel does not give the feeling of being restored or redone; rather it lets you easily slip back to 1893 when

The Nutt House

Period dining room

the hotel was built. Hood County was created primarily from Johnson County as an act of legislature in 1865. Jake and Jesse Nutt, two blind brothers, and a man named Lambert donated 40 acres as the county seat. After much argument from proponents of other sites, the Nutts' parcel was chosen and became Granbury, named for Confederate General Hiram Granbury. In 1866 the brothers built a 16 x 22-foot log cabin store on the site of the current Nutt House. It was Granbury's first store. In 1879, Jake and Jesse's younger brother, David Lee Nutt (Mary Lou's grandfather), built a house nearby, bringing cypress by oxcart from the East Texas forests. There were no hotels or restaurants in Granbury at the time, so David invited the drummers (traveling salesmen) to stay overnight at his home until they could catch the stagecoach the next day. His wife quickly had enough of the constant company and turned the house into a paying hotel and restaurant by adding a display room on the front and guest rooms in the back. The sleeping rooms were removed in the early 1900s after the hotel was built.

In 1893, in place of the log store, the Nutts had a stone and cypress structure built by a local contractor, Jim Warren, which became a new store, hotel, and restaurant. By the turn of the century, the hotel and restaurant were a favorite resting place for drummers, touring actors and actresses, and the townspeople, all called to meals by the same dinner bell that can be seen in the restaurant today. The train stopped a few blocks from the square, and mule hacks brought travelers to all-you-can-eat fare.

As any good town should, Granbury has many stories to pass on to new generations. In the late 1800s, there were five saloons on the square, and in 1870, a young man with a limp, John St. Helen, came to town and worked as a bartender in one of them. The story is that he became quite ill and confessed on what he thought was his deathbed about being John Wilkes

Booth. Upon recovery, he quickly left town. In 1938, workers razing a house where St. Helen had stayed found a derringer of the type that had killed Lincoln. It was wrapped in a newspaper with reports of the assassination. Who knows?

Carrie Nation came to Granbury in 1905. By the time she left in 1906, the saloons were gone. The town is still dry. Someone suggested that as the reason for the popularity of lemonade in Granbury. Every eating establishment serves excellent lemonade, most of it freshly squeezed.

Billy the Kid studied the violin as a boy in Granbury, and Belle Starr is said to have hid out once near here. Elizabeth Crockett, widow of Davy, moved to Granbury and is buried in the nearby Acton cemetery. Crockett descendants still live in Granbury. Another story is that Jesse James was buried in the Granbury cemetery on August 18, 1951. The coroner who examined him said that he had numerous bullet wound scars, and several of James' relatives were at the funeral to whisper their goodbyes. Who knows?

Mary Lou has tried to preserve the local art of folk cooking by serving the same type of meals cooked long ago, using some of the same recipes. She serves dinner (noon meal) daily and supper Thursday and Friday evenings, each one announced by the ringing of the dinner bell. Meals are family style at long tables, one of which is the old counter from the mercantile store, and high-backed oak chairs with carving across the back. There are meats, salads, relishes, buttermilk pie, and cobblers. Meals are first come, first served, and the line begins forming well in advance of the scheduled hours.

The Nutt House cooking has a following far from Granbury. In fact, the hot water cornbread caused a lively exchange of letters in a Dallas newspaper a few years ago. The reporter commented on the excellence of the cornbread, and in another article, he suggested that its creator ought to enter the state hush puppy contest. Letters came agreeing and asking for the recipe. There were more comments back and forth, with Mary Lou even sending in a letter saying that she had never heard anyone call her cornbread hush puppies, but that she had thought about the contest once, but didn't get around to it. Finally a reader ended the flow of letters by saying that with such a product there was obviously no reason to enter a contest, and Mary Lou eventually printed her recipe. If you look around the lobby, you will find it.

As in pre-air-conditioning days, a double screen door separates the lobby from the dining room for air flow and to keep out flies. One of the Dallas newspapers reported that the Presbyterians advertised in the local journal a new service beginning at 9:30 a.m. . . . so worshippers can beat the Baptists to the Nutt House for Sunday dinner.

The town square, of which the Nutt House is a part, is interesting and vibrant. The Merchant's Association has sensible rules for the merchants on the square. The result is a good mixture of shops, restaurants, and businesses which are enticing to tourists. Our hats are off to the citizens of Granbury, Mary Lou Watkins, and the Nutt House.

Reservations: (817) 573-5612. The Nutt House Hotel, Town Square, Granbury, Tx 76048. $12.84—single, $21.40—double, $32.10—suite, $5 each extra person, deposit required.

Directions: 35 miles southwest of Fort Worth on U.S. 377.

## POINTS OF INTEREST

The entire town square. Most of the buildings have historic markers with short descriptions of their history.

Lake Granbury — fishing lake created in 1970 by damming the Brazos River. 103-mile shoreline.

Hood County Jail — off the square, in use as a jail

Hood County Courthouse

Opera House on the square

until 1978, now being renovated for law offices. The hanging tower was never used.

Granbury Cemetery — Jesse James may be buried here.

Hood County Courthouse — center of town square.

Acton Cemetery — Elizabeth Crockett, wife of Davy, is buried here.

# The Woodbine

*Madisonville*

When John Parten was growing up in Madisonville he dreamed of buying the spectacular old Wills Hotel which was slowly deteriorating through neglect. John's family had lived in Madisonville for three generations, the earlier Partens remembering a time when the hotel was the town's social center and had its finest restaurant.

John was able to follow his dream in 1979, when he and his wife Lynne bought the Wills Hotel and began its renovation. Even though they hired a restoration manager, Joe Pinnelli, to plan and supervise the reconstruction, John and Lynne were up to their elbows in wiring and carpentry work. Lynne taught herself glass sandblasting and stained glass window making and she became quite knowledgeable about the history of wallpaper designs. She saved samples of the seven or eight layers of wallpaper that once covered the hotel walls in order to understand the mood and feeling of early 20th century designs. Each room of the hotel now has a different wallpaper; in fact many rooms have several patterns in the tradition of early 1900 design, very innovatively and attractively fitted together.

The restaurant was the first part of the hotel to open. "We're going to restore not only the atmosphere of the building, but the food as well," says Joe Pinnelli. "We would like someone to be able to walk back into 1904 and experience it all — cornbread, biscuits, and

The Woodbine

blackeyed peas. We're practically spending as much time recreating the menus of its early era as we have in restoring the building".

And what delicious meals the hotel serves: smoked ribs, fried chicken, baked ham, fresh garden vegetables, homemade breads, cakes, and cream pies, and large glasses of brewed ice tea. The meals are served at long tables, boarding house style. Perhaps the Partens hope that travelers will again remark, like Norman Kittrel did in 1921: "There is not a hotel in Texas today, barring none, that ever served such meals as were served in that interior hamlet (Madisonville)."

The guest rooms were completed in February of 1982. There are nine rooms, all upstairs. The hotel originally had 23 rooms, but many were small and without baths. Two of the guest rooms are large suites, one particularly lovely. It contains an octagonal turret with large windows on all sides. Breakfast is served in the upstairs lobby and consists of freshly-baked rolls, homemade jellies, and honey from the hives on the hotel property.

The Woodbine Hotel's original name was the Shapira Hotel, named for Jake and Sarah Shapira, Russian Jews, who emigrated to the U.S. in the late 19th century. They owned a dry goods store on Madisonville's town square and ran a saloon in back of the store. There Jake met the drummers or traveling salesmen who became his major clients for the boarding house he built on the back of the family home.

After the home burned in 1904, the oldest Shapira son, David, constructed the present building, which was named the Shapira Hotel. Jake Shapira died the following year, and the younger children and Mrs. Shapira took over its operation.

The Shapiras gave up their hotel in 1922, leasing it to various operators. It was sold to Clara Wills in 1929, at which time the name was changed to the Wills Hotel. Clara and her daughter Tommie continued the tradition

Hotel Lobby

Woodbine Dining Room

of serving fine family style meals, but the hotel eventually declined. The Wills continued to live in the hotel until 1978. It was sold to the Partens in 1979.

During the time the hotel was unoccupied, thieves took most of the original light fixtures and some of the furnishings. Vandals broke the remaining lights and some windows. The Partens have replaced all fixtures and are furnishing the hotel with some of its original pieces bought in an estate sale and with other antiques they have found around town.

The Partens are proud of their beautiful hotel and will gladly show you around the Woodbine. They like to point out its standing seam metal roof, pine staircase, and decorative plinth blocks above each doorway and window and the new peacock wallpaper in the upstairs lobby. They enjoy discussing all the construction and decorating decisions that have to be made and the difficulty in finding craftspeople who can duplicate 19th-century methods. They look forward to the day when the Woodbine, named after a native plant, will return to prominence as the main social center for Madisonville.

In 1980 the building was entered into the National Register of Historic Places.

Reservations: (713) 348-3591. 209 N. Madison, Madisonville, Texas 77864. $40 double, $75 for suite.

Directions: Madisonville is approximately 100 miles north of Houston on I-45. Take the Hwy. 21 West exit into Madisonville. Turn right at the third traffic light (on the square).

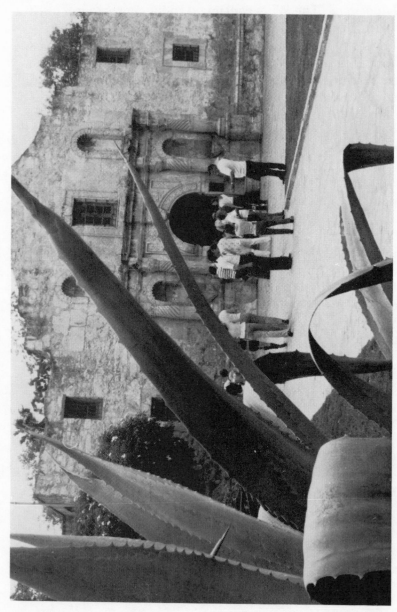

The Alamo

# Central Texas

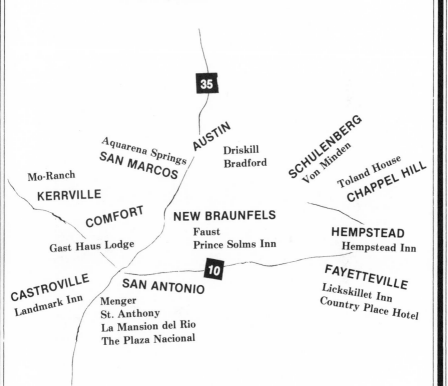

AUSTIN

**35**

Aquarena Springs
**SAN MARCOS**

Driskill
Bradford

**SCHULENBERG**
Von Minden

Toland House
**CHAPPEL HILL**

Mo-Ranch
**KERRVILLE**

**COMFORT**

**NEW BRAUNFELS**
Faust
Prince Solms Inn

**HEMPSTEAD**
Hempstead Inn

Gast Haus Lodge

**10**

**CASTROVILLE**
Landmark Inn

**SAN ANTONIO**
Menger
St. Anthony
La Mansion del Rio
The Plaza Nacional

**FAYETTEVILLE**
Lickskillet Inn
Country Place Hotel

The Driskill

# The Driskill

*Austin*

It is Monday morning at the Driskill, and the dining room is filled with legislators, lobbyists, state agency officials, and a sprinkling of convention people and tourists. Most of these convening for breakfast are male, well-dressed, talking politics, smoking, and drinking cup after cup of coffee. This scene has changed little since Colonel Jesse Driskill, one of the first Texas cattlemen to drive his cattle to the railheads of the North, opened the doors to the Driskill in 1886. He built the hotel so that visitors arriving by stagecoach or by horseback with saddlebags for luggage could have a first class place to stay.

And first class it was. Its exterior is ornate, Romanesque in style and built of brick covered with limestone. Outside cornices and trim are elaborately carved, and stone busts of the Driskill men are over the entrances; Jesse's likeness on the south side, his sons' over the east and west sides. The Pecan Street entrance was the largest arched doorway in Texas. The ladies' entrance on Brazos Street led directly to the elevator so women could avoid hearing the rough talk of the cattlemen in the lobby of the bar patrons. Several feet of cement were poured between each floor, making the Driskill almost fire proof.

The first floor of the Driskill consisted of a popular billiard room, a bar with a mounted Texas steer head, a barber shop, and rest rooms. The lobby floors were black slate and marble. The ceiling was 20 feet high, of corrugated sheet iron divided by strips of finely carved heart pine.

The second floor held the grand dining room, a ladies' dressing room, club dining room, children's dining room, men's parlor, ladies' parlor, two bridal apartments, and a large reading room for guests. The halls on all floors, some as wide as 35 feet, were designed to capture each breeze and circulate it through the hotel. The third and fourth floors contained guest rooms furnished with marble bureaus, wash stands, and carved walnut and cherry furniture. Heavy velvet carpets covered the floor, and lace draperies framed the windows. The chairs were covered with crushed velvet or with maroon leather.

The Driskill was designed by J. N. Preston and Sons, and the cost, including furniture, was $400,000. Not much today, but quite a fortune at the time. The building was heated by steam, and some guests enjoyed their first elevator ride at the Driskill. Needless to say, the opening of such an elaborate hotel was of statewide, even nationwide interest.

Five months after its opening, the Driskill was closed due to financial difficulties. It remained closed for many months before being purchased and reopened. This event was indicative of the many changes of ownership to come.

The next owner, Major George W. Littlefield, added electricity in 1895, making the Driskill the first hotel west of St. Louis to have electricity. In 1899, he set up his bank in the hotel, and the state's first interstate telephone line was installed in the Driskill. The newspapers reported that "A man can now talk to someone in Kansas City, St. Louis, or Chicago."

The Driskill was proud of its steam laundry and warned guests that a shirt would be ruined by two unprofessional launderings. Another service was Turkish baths, installed in 1909 to take advantage of the hot sulphur springs from the Driskill water wells.

As the Driskill moved through the century, events at the hotel mirrored the circumstances of the times. In 1917 and 1918, there were draft card checks at the hotel, as in all other hotels across the country. A man caught without his draft card would be sent straight to the recruiting office.

When the Depression came and Roosevelt declared a bank holiday, people were frantic upon discovering they had no way to get cash. The Driskill management went to the safe and quietly passed out money to the needy guests. Every last penny was repaid when the hometown banks finally reopened. In the same year, Austin's first fire department, named the Driskill Fire Department, was organized at the hotel.

In 1930, a 15-story annex was added to the hotel, complete with a penthouse apartment. Rooms are now available in either the old section (the traditional section, as Driskill management prefers to call it) or the new. Most rooms in the old section contain antiques, although most are not the original furnishings. These were sold by auction in 1969. Since then, management has been slowly reacquiring some of these treasures, some given back, and others bought back. Most of the rooms are large and quite comfortable, and guests enjoy wandering throughout this ornate hotel inspecting each nook and cranny.

The ballrooms and meeting rooms are elaborately decorated. The Maximilian Room has a particularly poignant story to tell. Carlotta, daughter of King Leopold of Belgium, and Maximilian, Archduke of Austria, were married in 1861. His present to Carlotta was eight gold leaf framed mirrors with a gilt medallion of her, reputed to be the most beautiful woman in Europe, at the top of each one. In 1863 Maximilian was installed as emperor of Mexico by Napoleon III. After arriving, they discovered that almost the entire North American continent was disturbed with political unrest, soon culminating in the

113

revolution for the independence of Mexico. When French troops withdrew from Mexico, Maximilian decided to remain. With Maximilian's life in danger, Carlotta fled back to Europe to seek aid for her husband. Her unsuccessful attempts drove her insane, and she remained in Europe in seclusion until her death in 1928. Maximilian was court-martialed and faced the firing squad in 1867. His body was returned to Vienna for state burial. The mirrors were brought to San Antonio for safekeeping and remained in storage there until 1930, when the Driskill bought them and hung them in a room specially decorated to display the mirrors, which they named the Maximilian Room.

The Driskill Hotel has always been associated with politicians. Governors began giving their inaugural balls there in 1887, just one year after it opened. The Texas state capitol building, with the tallest dome in the United States, was built two years after the Driskill and is within walking distance. In 1908, the Driskill arranged to receive the national election returns. They were thrown by steropticon onto the wall of the building across the street while people placed bets in the bar. The hotel was headquarters for the White House when Lyndon Johnson was in Texas. The Driskill has been lucky for almost all politicians who have held their elections return gathering there, and legend has it that Lady Bird and Lyndon Johnson met for breakfast there on their first date. The Driskill Hotel reflects the makeup of the city as few others do — politicians, university people, artists, and tourists.

Reservations: (512) 474-5911. 117 East 7th Street, Austin, Texas 78701. Rates: $50 up for a double. Check for weekend specials.


Directions: Take the 6th Street exit off Interstate Highway 35. Turn west on 6th Street towards the downtown area. Turn right on Congress; then turn right onto 7th Street.

## POINTS OF INTEREST

Elizabeth Ney Museum. Houses art treasure of world renown-sculptor, Elizabeth Ney. 44th and Avenue H.

Governor's Mansion. White Greek Revival mansion built in 1856, filled with antique furnishings. Public rooms are open for a few hours daily. 1010 Colorado Street.

Lyndon B. Johnson Library. Archives and museum related to LBJ and the presidential office. Particularly interesting are the gifts to LBJ from foreign heads of state and from U.S. citizens. 2300 Red River Street.

State Capitol Complex. 46 acres of landscaped grounds, plus the Capitol, a classic statehouse of Texas pink granite. Tourist Information Center operated by State Department of Highways and Public Transportation gives out information about the Capitol, Austin, and Texas.

State Cemetery. Monuments mark the graves of approximately 2,000 patriots, statesmen, and heroes of Texas, including the tomb of Stephen F. Austin.

Parks. Eight large parks, including Long Lake Metropolitan Park, Blue Bluff Road, Fiesta Gardens on Town Lake, Lake Austin Metropolitan Park.

St. David's Episcopal Church. Oldest Protestant church west of the Mississippi, completed in 1854.

French Legation. Built in 1840 by French charge d'affaires to the Republic of Texas. Contains period furnishings. 817 E. 8th St.

The State Capitol

# Bradford
# Hotel

The Bradford Austin is the new name of the old Stephen F. Austin Hotel, one block west of the Driskill on Congress Avenue. The Stephen F. Austin was developed in the early 1920s by the Chamber of Commerce, which had seen the city suffer through several years of hotel room shortages. An agreement was drawn up for the Austin citizens to buy $600,000 worth of bonds and T. B. Baker of Baker Hotels to build a hotel of not less that 200 rooms.

Each party met its obligations, and on May 19, 1924, the Stephen F. Austin opened its doors. It had 250 rooms and a foundation capable of supporting seven more floors. The hotel had all the conveniences that a 1920s hotel would have: ice water running through the plumbing system, a bath in each guest room, closets, plus a supply closet where guests could get what they needed without interacting with hotel employees. A grand marble staircase graced the lobby, and there were fine Persian carpets.

The hotel was named after Texas' most admired statesman, Stephen F. Austin, who did more than any other to settle Texas. It was to have been called The Texas until the local Business Women's Club lobbied to have its name changed to honor a Texas hero.

Soon after the opening, the hotel's Roof Garden on

the tenth floor became a popular place for Austin's high society. The Roof Garden, with glass on all sides, was phased out when five floors were added in 1938 under Conrad Hilton's ownership. Over the years, the Stephen F. Austin served the purpose for which it was designed. Legislators and lobbyists met here, as did business associations and tourists who enjoyed the hotel's quiet atmosphere. Eventually, however, the Stephen F. Austin took the downhill path of so many city hotels.

Fortunately, the Stephen F. Austin is being rescued by the Kerr Corporation of Minnesota. The hotel re-opened in January, 1982 after a thorough renovation.

Reservations: (512) 476-4361. 701 Congress Avenue, Austin, Texas, 78701. $65 up for a double.

Directions: Take the 6th Street exit on I-35. Turn west on 6th Street, then turn right on Congress Avenue. The Bradford Austin is across the street from the new wing of the Driskill and a few blocks west of I-35.

## POINTS OF INTEREST

See Points of Interest for the Driskill Hotel.

# Aquarena Springs Inn

## San Marcos

Aquarena Springs was built on the San Marcos River headwaters, which are now called Spring Lake. A.B. Rogers purchased 125 acres of the property in March 1926, and on April 21, 1928, opened Springlake Hotel and golf course. The springs, which maintain a year round temperature of 71°, had a number of swimming novelties, such as a water slide, a spinning top, and an elevator for underwater photography. Big band names provided music for rooftop dancing. The current manager, Gene Phillips, remembers sitting on the hill as a boy and watching the dances.

With the onset of the Depression, Rogers had to close the hotel, leasing it to doctors as a medical clinic and health spa. In 1940 he leased it to the Brown School for Handicapped Children. In 1946, A.B.'s son, Paul, built his first glass-bottomed boat in an old rowboat for the school, and in 1951, he started the Aquarena Submarine Theater. A.B. died in 1953, but Paul continued ownership.

When Brown School moved out in 1961, Paul refurbished the hotel and reopened the resort to the public, to the delight of those who remembered it from its early days. At the first glimpse of the hotel, you know you have arrived at a real resort. The buildings are sparkling white, the grass is green, there is a large swimming pool and lake, and people are playing golf. The inn is a long two-story white stucco building which has 25 rooms,

Aquarena Springs

with the springs on the front side. The small space at the back between the building and the cliffs has been enclosed to contain plants, parakeets, and pigeons. The rooms are ordinary, but neat and comfortable. Their most delightful aspect is the patios. They look out either over the water or the garden aviary and are wonderful for sitting and watching the activity.

Aquarena Springs has something for everyone. There is golf, swimming in the Olympic-size pool, hiking in the wooded hills, strolling the well-maintained landscape, feeding the ducks and geese, eating in the good restaurant, visiting the grist mill, store, museum, and reconstructed buildings, or being entertained at several shows and attractions.

The various entertainments are all interesting, but the glass-bottomed boats are truly enchanting. They glide above hundreds of high pressure springs and skim over the masses of aquatic vegetation which grow back quickly after being cut and sent to fish supply stores.

Another well-known attraction is the Submarine Theatre which holds 275 people per show. It had sea lions at one time and now has a swimming pig. The area used to be a swimming pool with a swing out over the water, and has been the scene of an underwater wedding.

When walking in the hills above the springs, it is easy to imagine what the area was like when the founders of San Marcos lived there. General Edward Burleson came to Bastrop in 1830 with Stephen F. Austin's second colony. In 1845, he acquired 340 acres including the headwaters of the San Marcos River and what is now downtown San Marcos. By 1848, his family had settled in the hill overlooking present-day Aquarena Springs.

Burleson was a prominent figure in Texas' battle for independence and was a vice president of the Republic of Texas and a state legislator. With two other landowners, he designed the town of San Marcos. The houses belonging to the Burlesons and one of the other landowners

Patio of Aquarena Springs Inn

Burleson Dog Run House

have been reconstructed on their original sites on the Aquarena Springs property. The Burleson Dog Run House was reconstructed in 1964 with the original chimney stones and logs from buildings for the same period. Burleson also built a sawmill, gristmill, and cotton gin over the springs to operate by water power. A grist mill can be seen today at the site of the original mill. Between the houses and the mill are the remains of a Spanish mission, left from missionaries who came to the area in the 1700s.

The atmosphere of the inn is quiet and relaxing and a wonderland for children. In fact, much of the business is repeat business. People who came here as children are bringing their own children back, and anniversaries are celebrated here. The rooms are comfortable, and the grounds are beautiful with tall cypress trees, oak, elephant ears, and a variety of flowers. It is easy to see why there is so much repeat business.

Reservations: (512) 392-2481. P.O. Box 2330, San Marcos, Tx 78666. $30 single, $30-48 double. Room service 7:30 a.m.-10 p.m., hot water maker in room for instant coffee or tea. No pets. Combination ticket to all attractions, $7.95. Iron and ironing boards available at front desk.

Directions: I-35 to San Marcos. Follow the signs to Aquarena Springs.

### POINTS OF INTEREST

Wonder World—Wonder Cave, near Aquarena Springs, a Texas historical site. Open year round. Get directions at desk, or I-35, Redwood exit.

Republic of Texas Chilympiad—third weekend in Sept. in San Marcos.

Manor House

*Photo courtesy of the Mo-Ranch*

# Mo-Ranch

## Hunt

The traveler in the Hill County has a treat in store at
the Mo-Ranch. There is swimming in the north fork of
the Guadalupe River, playing in the rapids, canoeing,
boating, fishing, golfing, ping-pong, basketball,
volleyball, tennis, jogging, hiking, or birdwatching.
Bring your own equipment. Overnight guests will share
the place with convention members, since the ranch is
also a conference center, attended for the most part by
religious groups. The conference facilities are not
restricted to religious groups, however, and offer an attractive alternative to the cocktail conventions in the
midst of a bustling city.

O. R. Seagraves, an oilman, built a large stone house
on the property in 1929. The river was dammed and a
dock constructed. The Depression brought financial difficulties, forcing Seagraves to sell the property in 1936.
The 6,800 acres and house were sold to a friend, Daniel J.
Moran, president of Continental Oil Company.

For the next eleven years Moran supervised a pro-
digious amount of building. He had an appreciation of
native materials and a good sense of style and place-
ment, resulting in a pleasing blend of buildings with the
surrounding hills and river. The buildings are constructed for the most part with local limestone and cedar
and are unobtrusively connected with paths and
walkways. Oil pipe was available from Moran's company, which he sometimes disguised as cedar in roof sup-

Guest Lodge

*Photo courtesy of the Mo-Ranch*

ports. Look for these in the ceiling of the chapel and try to tell which are pipe and which are wood.

The Mo-Ranch signature is everywhere, incorporated into the design of a floor, inscribed in glass balls in fireplaces, and set in tile in the swimming pool. The fireplaces are another unusual aspect of Mo-Ranch. Each one is different, some seeming to grow out of the wall itself. Some are embedded with decorations of wood, tile, glass, petrified wood, rocks, and gemstones.

The pool next to the Manor House was added in 1938, with over two million hand-set tiles. It is connected to the Manor House with a limestone walkway with iron grillwork and a red tile roof, complementing the house nicely. The house itself is made of limestone with hardwood floors and is adorned with wrought iron, a red tile roof, and the numerous fireplaces. The chapel, with its beautiful stained glass windows, was built in 1941 for some Roman Catholic priests who would accompany the Moran family to the ranch from the St. Thomas School in Houston. Loma Linda Lodge was built for a projected scout camp which never materialized. The priests operated the lodge as a camp for boys in the summers of 1944-1946. The stained glass scenes at the lodge represent Girl and Boy Scout activities.

Also constructed were an ice plant, a gymnasium featuring a huge roller skating rink, dormitories, a barn, and bridges across the river and a gulch. A conservatory-greenhouse was brought from Oklahoma and placed across from the pool. Today plants in the conservatory are for sale, and there is a small aviary to one side for canaries and parakeets.

In 1947, Moran had to discontinue construction due to illness, and in 1949 he sold the ranch to the Synod of Red River Presbyterian Church. They in turn sold most of the land to the State of Texas, keeping 377 acres, the buildings, and the name. (The complete name became Presbyterian Mo-Ranch Assembly.) The land sold to the

State of Texas is now known as the Kerr Wildlife Management Area.

In 1952, a large dining hall was added, which also houses a bookstore and canteen. In 1958, a two-story motel called Pheasant Run was built, acquiring its name from the cement foundations of the old pheasant cages upon which it was constructed. More classrooms were built, nature trails established, and playgrounds added.

The Nicklos Place, a more recent addition, was acquired from a friend of Moran. It is used as a retreat for up to 30 adults (no children). The barn and chicken house have been made into a home for the director of the Nicklos Place. Visitors should respect the privacy of the center, but are welcome to walk up the road to the right of the property to the outdoor cross and benches and a spectacular view of the ranch lands and river below. All buildings except the Nicklos Place are open to guests.

Reservations must be made at least a week in advance, and meals must be ordered at the same time. The meals are convenient, but unless you are nostalgic for summer camp food, a better suggestion is to drive to town, or bring your own ice chest and have picnics. The ranch is often full in the summer, especially on weekends, so plan on visiting September through March. The Manor House is definitely the first choice of accommodations. The rooms are cozy, with wood floors and working fireplaces. Each has a door opening onto a balcony for an excellent view of the river below. Unless traveling with a large group, the other choice is Pheasant Run, which is a standard motel, but which has balconies with benches for viewing the countryside.

There are several nature trails with pamphlets to point out attractions along the way. One of the trails goes past a limestone cliff where primitive Indians cooked their meals. Another trail leads down to a clear cool creek and past an old shooting range. Bird watching is excellent, and at the right time of the year there should be deer, armadillos, and rabbits. An altogether pleasant

Guadalupe River

place to be. Dan Moran's joy of life, imagination, and love of nature are evident in his Mo-Ranch.

Reservations: (512) 238-4455. Hunt, Tx., 78024. $20—single, $24—double, $27—triple, $29—quadruple, $2 campground, $6.75—R.V. hookups. No pets. Reservations must be made one week in advance. Closed Dec. 15—Jan. 1.

Directions: I-10 to Kerrville, west on Tx 27 to Ingram, west on Tx 39 to Hunt, then west on FM 1340 to Mo-Ranch.

The Gast Haus Lodge

# The Gast
# Haus Lodge

## Comfort

Frederick Christian Meyer, a wheelwright, came to Comfort in 1862 to manage the town's first stage stop and weigh station (built in 1857). There was a small log cabin to which he added a second story. In 1869, he built a rock house for his wife and future family. There they raised eight children and rented the upstairs rooms to stagecoach passengers. In 1872 they built two wooden structures directly behind the stage stop for maternity rooms. Frederick's wife, Ernestine Mueller, was a midwife who needed the rooms for the women of the surrounding area ranches. The Honeymoon Cottage was built that same year in the back of the property near the banks of Cypress Creek to accommodate additional stagecoach passengers.

In 1887, the railroad lines were completed, and Comfort became a resort community. That year the Meyers expanded the complex by building the current White House as a hotel. They met guests from San Antonio and Kerrville at the train station and took them back to the hotel by carriage, where they could have a bountiful 50¢ dinner in the dining room or have a picnic on the grassy banks of the river. The passengers would then either go back by return train or remain overnight. By this time, all of the buildings in the complex were being used for overnight guests.

Stage stop built in 1851

Cypress Creek at the Gast Haus Lodge

In 1889, Frederick Meyer died, leaving Ernestine and the eight children to operate the hotels and restaurant. After Ernestine died in 1910, one of the daughters, Julia, married a man from Galveston named Ellenburger. Julia and her husband managed the complex with some help from the other Meyer children. Comfort remained a resort; the guests would come from as far away as Houston and Beaumont, remaining for the entire summer.

Apparently Julia Ellenburger was quite a character who ran her complex of rooms well and served delicious meals. Business was so good that in 1920 a stucco hotel was added. The two rooms available today for overnight guests are in the top floor of this building. The rooms are airy and spacious, with 12-foot ceilings and large windows. The back room is a sleeping porch and also has a kitchen area with a stove, refrigerator, sink, and cabinets. Decorations are plain but pleasant, with current magazines on the bedside table. There is a constant breeze, but guests may experience some discomfort from the heat on summer evenings. There is a gas space heater for winter chills.

Guests are welcome to wander around the grounds, but should remember that all the buildings except for the hotel are rented by permanent lodgers. Look for the hoist on the second-floor balcony of the White House, which was used to lift boarders' trunks to the second story. The covered well to the right of the front door was dug by hand and is still in use. The small building behind the hotel was a detached kitchen. Ask directions to the swimming and fishing area farther down the road from the Gast Haus Lodge.

When Julia died in 1956, ownership passed to the Lutheran Church, which continued to operate the establishment. They added a large, tree-shaded swimming pool in the early '60s. Ann McGrath purchased the complex in 1973. When she took possession, she discovered that all the beautiful old furniture acquired by the Meyers and Ellenbergers was gone. She managed to open the complex to overnight and permanent lodgers anyway, and then had to contend with another crisis in the severe flood of 1978. Water and mud rose several feet in the buildings nearest the creek, but none of them were structurally damaged.

Over the year, Ann has gradually reduced the number of overnight accommodations to the two in the stucco building. She would like to convert these to permanent lodging also, but is keeping them because she thinks Comfort should be able to offer lodging to visitors.

The town of Comfort is very interesting, and its entire downtown is listed in the National Register of Historic Places. The first Sundays in June and December are open houses sponsored by the Creative Arts of Comfort.

Reservations: (512) 995-2304. Comfort, Texas 78012. $40. Deposit plus expected time of arrival required.

Directions: Comfort is located on I-10. 51 miles northwest of San Antonio.

## POINTS OF INTEREST

Find a brochure in one of the downtown stores for the walking tour.

# The Menger Hotel

*San Antonio*

William A. Menger was born in Germany on March 15, 1827. He emigrated to the United States in 1847 and became an American citizen in 1852. His trades were that of cooper and brewer, and after arriving in San Antonio, he continued to practice these trades. He opened Menger Brewery in 1855 on the grounds of the Alamo Battle. The beer was chilled in the huge cellars of the brewery located on Alamo Plaza at the site of the present Menger Hotel. The cellars had walls of stone three feet thick which are now the basement of the Menger Hotel, and which were cooled by the Alamo Madre ditch flowing through what is now the patio of the Menger Hotel. The brewery was immediately successful.

Mary Baumschlueter emigrated from Germany with her mother in 1846. After arriving in Galveston on a freight schooner from Hamburg, they took a small boat up Buffalo Bayou to Harrisburg, near what is now the port of Houston. Here they camped for two weeks waiting for a conveyance to San Antonio. The trip over land took six weeks by ox cart, and only the hearty survived such trips. Mary's mother died soon after arriving in San Antonio and Mary was sick for a year. She married a man named Guenther. When he died, she opened a boarding house at St. Mary's and Commerce. William Menger was one of the patrons of her establishment, and in 1851, William and Mary were married.

William and Mary continued to run the boarding

The Menger Hotel

house for a short while until it became so popular that in 1855 they built a larger boarding house next to the brewery. The plank boarding house became even more popular than the one the Mengers had outgrown. The brewery and boarding house attracted old German farmers from Fredericksburg, New Braunfels, and Seguin who arrived by oxcart and needed a place to stay for the night. The U.S. Army was stationed in San Antonio, creating a large demand for boarding houses. San Antonio was also the biggest stagecoach stop between New Orleans and San Diego, with three stage lines going through the city.

With such a large demand for rooms, the Mengers soon announced plans to replace their boarding house with a "large and commodious hotel". Stone was quarried for the hotel from what is now the beautiful Sunken Gardens in Brackenridge Park. The two-story hotel which was connected to the brewery opened February 1, 1859, 23 years after the Battle of the Alamo. It was built by J.H. Kampmann at a cost of approximately $16,000. Spanish in style, with iron grill work, it had 50 rooms and a well-ventilated stone stable for travelers' horses.

Many townspeople thought the Mengers were foolish to build a fine hotel away from Military Plaza and Main Plaza. But instead of being foolish, it turned the tide of business toward Alamo Plaza, which at the time contained little more than the brewery and a crumbling old mission destined to be Texas' greatest shrine.

The Menger was an elegant hotel, one of few such places in the western U.S. at the time. It was much too expensive a place for the average traveler who bunked down in the wagon yard on Blum Street near the Menger. For the wealthy and famous, however, it was a favorite stopping place. Captain Richard King, of the King Ranch family, retained a room at the Menger, and when he died, had his funeral there. Oscar Wilde stayed there, as did O. Henry, Frances Parkinson Keyes, and Sidney Lanier, a popular 19th-century poet and song

A journey into the past

writer. The opera singer Jenny Lind stayed there while performing at the opera house across the plaza, as did actresses Sarah Bernhardt and Lily Langtry.

The Menger's dining room served only the finest delicacies: buffalo hump and tongue, wild turkey, deer loins, and soup made of San Antonio river turtle, and for dessert, their own creation, mango ice cream. The menu for Christmas dinner in 1893 is representative of the cuisine that made the hotel famous. It included oysters, whitefish, sirloin of beef, Yorkshire pudding, mallard duck, currant jelly, suckling pig stuffed with oysters, turkey with chestnut dressing, orange fritters, English plum pudding, boned turkey in aspic, asparagus, cauliflower, and new peas.

In 1871, William Menger died, so Mary continued to run the hotel until 1881 when it was sold to Major J.H. Kampmann. The military telegraph line was brought to San Antonio in 1875, and the train came in 1877. On the afternoon of February 19, 1877, the Galveston-Harrisburg-San Antonio Railway steamed into San Antonio. The city had a torchlight parade through the town to Alamo Plaza with a celebration lasting three days. The Menger hung Chinese lanterns from cornices and every window. It was said that whenever the train pulled into town, the passengers raced to the Menger to get first choice of one of the eight rooms with a bath.

In 1890, the famous Menger bar was added, a replica of the bar in the House of Lord's Club in London. The bar was solid cherry, with a cherry paneled ceiling, French mirrors, and gold-plated spittoons. It was the marvel of San Antonio. Mint juleps were served in solid silver tumblers, and hot rum toddies were popular. The procurement of ice for the bar gives hint as to the difficulty of running a sophisticated hotel in frontier Texas. The ice was shipped from Boston to Indianola, then carted to San Antonio in specially made wagons.

In 1898, Teddy Roosevelt visited this bar when he came to the Menger Hotel as co-organizer of the First

U.S. Volunteer Cavalry, later called the Rough Riders, a name coined in San Antonio. They chose San Antonio as the gathering place because it was in good horse country, near the Gulf, it was an arsenal, and it was an army post. He recruited many of the men in the Menger Bar, saying "I need a few good men who can ride a horse, shoot a gun, and want to serve their country". The heroes of San Juan Hill signed up.

The Menger was San Antonio's most prestigious hotel in the nineteenth century, but in the 1930s and 1940s it was allowed to decline to poor condition. The hotel went up for sale and the buyers planned to turn it into a parking lot. A huge protest arose over one of Texas' oldest and historically most important hotels. J. Frank Dobie was probably the most eloquent of the Menger's supporters. In his newspaper articles he explained how the Menger belonged to Alamo Plaza and to Texans everywhere — "belongs as quietly and as rightly as the evening star belongs to after-twilight, something settled and in harmony with itself in this screeching world of ceaseless change".

The advocates of the Menger won, and W.L. Moody, Jr. of Galveston purchased the Menger in 1943 from the Kampmann family for $205,000. After the purchase, all rooms were remodeled and new baths added. Atlee and Robert Ayres were the architects for the four-story, 125-room addition which brought the total room count to 225. This addition extended the Menger to Crockett Street. The new air-conditioned lobby was glassed in to look out on a patio filled with retama, palm, and banana trees. The bar was moved to the Crockett Street side, its importance diminished in modern days. This addition opened in 1950. The Ayres were also the architects when the Menger Patio Club and swimming pool were added in 1953.

In 1966-67, in preparation for HemisFair '68, a five-story addition at Crockett and Bonham Streets was begun for $1.5 million. This included 111 guest rooms and a motor lobby, again by architects Atlee and Robert Ayres. This brought the total of rooms to 327, and finally the Menger Hotel, now over 100 years old, occupied the entire block.

The Menger no longer serves buffalo tongue or river turtle, but it still offers mango ice cream and is a wonderfully situated hotel for jaunts to the many delightful sites of downtown San Antonio. Its old three-story lobby topped by stained glass is still a beauty and often takes the unknowing guest by surprise. The Menger Coffee Shop serves an outstanding breakfast and the Menger Restaurant a decent dinner. The hotel is not what it once was in terms of service, glamour, and cuisine, but it is an interesting journey into Texas' past.

Reservations: (512) 223-4361. 204 Alamo Plaza, San Antonio, Tx. 78298. Rates are $50 up for a double.

Directions: From IH-37/IH-35, follow the directions for the Alamo. The hotel is next to the Alamo.

## POINTS OF INTEREST

See the Points of Interest for the St. Anthony Hotel in San Antonio.

St. Anthony Hotel

# St. Anthony Hotel

## San Antonio

The St. Anthony is an elegant and richly furnished hotel in downtown San Antonio. It is filled with antique and modern art which includes Ming vases, Mexican wood sculptures, Mexican tile, wrought ironwork, and murals. The north side of the lobby, called Peacock Alley, is decorated with oriental rugs, eight-foot Empire-styled chandeliers, and a 1924 Steinway rosewood piano from France, originally made for the Russian Embassy in Washington. R.W. Morrison, the hotel's second owner, purchased the piano in 1936. The piano is not just collecting dust; in the evenings it is played for the benefit of bar and lobby guests.

St. Anthony's was built in 1909 by two wealthy cattlmen, A.H. Jones and B.L. Taylor. They picked a central site which they felt would grow into a large metropolitan area. St. Anthony's was the first hotel in the world to have central air-conditioning, electronic eye doors, and a completely equipped drive-in and garage registration facility. The hotel has been continually remodeled and improved and has tripled in size.

The hotel's 400 rooms are a variety of styles and sizes; all are tastefully furnished in fine furniture, quality draperies, and brass lamps. Plumbing hardware and fixtures were custom made for the bathrooms, and the bath tiles are of a unique flat style no longer possible to duplicate. There are several large, elegant formal entertaining and meeting rooms.

St. Anthony's has several bars and restaurants. The

143

The Garden Room

Spanish-style Garden Room serves meals all day, but is so bright and cheerful that it is particularly nice for breakfast. The hotel has a tobacco shop, a drug and liquor store, a gift shop, and fine art gallery. Valet and laundry services are also available.

The St. Anthony has followed the same development pattern as many other fine old hotels. It was once the gathering place or home of the very wealthy. Over a period of time its clients changed due to competition and other factors, so that now it is mainly patronized by the average tourist with a romantic bent.

Reservations: (512) 227-4392 or Texas toll free 1-800-292-5882, U.S. toll free 1-800-831-5766. 300 E. Travis, San Antonio, 78205. Rates are $80 up for doubles. Special weekend rates are sometimes available.

Directions: St. Anthony's is in downtown San Antonio on Travis Street.

## POINTS OF INTEREST

San Antonio has so many fascinating places to visit that they cannot all be listed here. For a more complete list and a map, write for the "Visitor's Map of San Antonio", P.O. Box 2277, San Antonio, 78298.

These places are within walking distance of the downtown hotels:

The Alamo. Texas' most famous historical shrine where approximately 180 men chose to die fighting rather than to surrender to several thousand soldiers under Mexican General Santa Anna. Among the Alamo dead were William Travis, Davy Crockett, and Jim Bowie. The Alamo was the church building of Mission San Antonio de Valero, first of the five Spanish colonial missions established in San Antonio in the early 18th century to Christianize and control the Indians. The mission was established in 1718; the church structure which today stands in downtown San Antonio was begun around

1755. It was during February and March of 1836 that this heroic battle took place.

Spanish Governor's Palace. In 1772 San Antonio became the seat of Spanish government in Texas with headquarters at the 10-room Spanish Governor's Palace on Military Plaza. Moses Austin came here in 1820 to ask for permission to bring a colony of U.S. citizens to Spanish Texas. Jim Bowie courted his aristocratic future wife here in 1830. The building is colonial Spanish in style; the building and its furnishings are well-preserved.

Paseo del Rio. The Riverwalk, with cafes, restaurants, hotels, and tropical foliage below street level.

HemisFair Plaza. Site of the 1968 Texas World's Fair. Some of the structures retained are the 750-foot Tower of the Americas with dining levels at 550 and 560 feet, topped by an observation deck offering panoramic views of the city. Open daily are the San Antonio Museum of Transportation, the Hall of Texas History, and the Institute of Texan Cultures which depicts the contributions of many cultural groups to Texas. Also in the Plaza are food stands, an aerial tramway, a monorail, a Philippine restaurant, and amusement rides.

Mexican Market. Small shops and stalls of local and imported Mexican handicrafts. Santa Rosa and Commerce streets.

The B and T Fuller Double-Decker Bus Company. English double-decker sightseeing buses have various tours which visit historical and modern places of interest in San Antonio seven days a week. Tours are accessible for handicapped persons. Tour buses load passengers at the Alamo. (512) 734-8706.

These sites are a short drive from the downtown hotels.

Brackenridge Park. A 343-acre park with picnic grounds, a skyride, and stables. The San Antonio Zoo, one of the world's finest, is also in the park, as is the Witte Memorial Museum, particularly famous for its Texana exhibits. 3903 N. St. Mary's Street.

Missions of San Antonio. In addition to the Alamo, four other missions were established in this area in the early 18th century.

Mission Nuestra Senora de la Purisma Concepcion. Established in 1731; completed in 1755.

Mission San Francisco de la Espada. Established in 1731. Church building is still in use, as is the irrigation system.

Mission San Jose y San Miguel de Aguayo. The "queen of missions" was founded in 1720; the church constructed between 1768-82. The entire compound, including the Indian dwellings, granary, and workshops, have been restored. The grounds contain the first flour mill built in Texas (1790). This mission is particularly famous for the richly carved facade of the church, including the sculptured exterior of the sacristy window known as the "Rose Window" or "Rosa's Window". The church's stone carvings are considered to be the finest Spanish ornamentation in the United States. The missions are located along Mission Road.

McNay Art Institute. Contains works of major 20th-century artists. 6000 N. New Braunfels Street.

La Mansion del Rio

# La Mansion Del Rio

## San Antonio

La Mansion del Rio has a perfect location. It over-looks the Paseo del Rio or Riverwalk, with its cafes, craft shops, theatres, restaurants, and attractive landscaping. The Paseo del Rio makes downtown San Antonio so in-viting that you might think this is some new project to revitalize a city's downtown area. Not so; the Riverwalk was begun in the 1920s by Robert Hugman, the city ar-chitect, who imagined that the downtown section of the San Antonio River could be something other than the bad-smelling, trash-filled ditch that it was. Its banks were lined with ramshackle back doors of buildings and trash heaps where rats lived. Flash flooding had citizens talking about filling up the downtown channel.

Robert Hugman thought the river could be clean, free of rubbish, and lined with trees and shrubs. It could have flights of stairs leading down from every street bridge to a stone walk along the river bank. Along the walk would be a variety of shops. Hugman carried sketches of the proposed riverwalk to civic groups who agreed the plans were attractive and possible, but no one would back the plans. The Depression was beginning, and the project sounded too expensive. The plans lay dormant until 1935 when Jack White, a hotel manager, saw Hugman's sketches. Jack White dedicated himself to seeing that the plans for the river became reality. Civic leaders and the citizens of San Antonio could not ignore his enthusiasm.

White spent an enormous amount of time convincing the property owners along the river of the benefits of spending money on the project. Finally, several of them agreed to pay $2.50 per frontage foot to help pay for the project. After that, property owners passed a tax assessment bill in 1938 to establish funds for the river project. The Work Projects Administration became involved, and a matching federal grant of $325,000 was set up. After four years of hard selling, White turned the first soil in the ground-breaking ceremonies held March 25, 1939. A few days later, the river's channel was drained, and a large crew of craftsmen began their works as stone masons, carpenters, painters, plasterers, engineers, and landscape architects. By the end of 1939, their work began to take shape. A variety of designs was developed. Walks are of flagstone, cobblestone, cement inlaid with pebbles, brick, and concrete patterns. Parts of the walk are inscribed with stars, circles, squares, and diagonals.

Nursery workers planted many species of subtropical plants; banana trees, pink crepe myrtle trees, yellow retamas, blue plumbago bushes, orange pomegranates, and graceful willows. Red cannas bloom in the summer, poinsettias in the winter. The floral pattern of the river is in harmony with the architectural design.

The Riverwalk has changed some over the years; lighting has been added for the safety and enjoyment of night strollers. Many shops, restaurants, and hotels have been built. Touring barges and paddleboats are available for rides down the river. However, the Riverwalk's essential enchanting quality is unchanged.

Many of La Mansion's rooms have balconies which overlook this attractive scene. From the Riverwalk, La Mansion del Rio has a very striking appearance with its white arched portals and iron balustrades. Spanish in style, the building has a central patio which contains a cafe and a swimming pool.

La Mansion has not always been Spanish nor has it

always been a hotel. La Mansion del Rio was once St. Mary's College, established in 1852 by four Frenchmen, members of the Society of Mary. Construction of St. Mary's began in 1852, and its doors opened in 1853 to more than 100 students. The structure then had four rooms.

In 1854, Brothers Eligius Beyrer and Charles Francis joined the faculty. Francis, known as "the Great Builder" was heavily involved in the development of San Antonio for 54 years. During this period, he finished the construction of the college. By 1870 the college was an attractive European-styled limestone structure. The limestone came from France. It was used as ballast in ships traveling to Indianola and was transported by wagons to San Antonio.

San Antonio is famous as a city of historic struggles. These brothers' struggle was also miraculous. They attempted to establish a first-rate school with frontier Texans as their students, and succeeded. For several decades, former students of St. Mary's dominated local business and civic affairs. Eight mayors of San Antonio attended St. Mary's. St. Mary's is the only college to have served the city for 113 consecutive years.

In 1966, the building was acquired by La Mansion Motor Hotel. A six-story addition was built facing the Riverwalk, and the hotel exterior was made Spanish in style by the addition of balconies and iron grillwork.

Most of La Mansion's rooms were built during the last decade in a modern style so are not nostalgic or reminiscent of earlier days. The rooms are spacious, modern, and clean and are furnished in a Spanish motif with high-back chairs, brightly colored bedspreads and ironwork decorative pieces. All rooms have a wall of real brick, exposed wooden ceiling beams, and double doors opening onto a balcony or walkway overlooking a patio or the Riverwalk. The hotel garage is connected to the building, which makes moving suitcases easier.

A room facing the Riverwalk would be nice during

Fiesta week in the spring and during Las Luminarias (the Festival of Lights) in December. Las Luminarias is a Mexican Christmas celebration. Children carrying candles walk the Riverwalk singing English and Spanish carols. The trees and buildings along the Riverwalk are decorated with Christmas lights. For these events, reservations should be made several months in advance.

In late 1979, a new 173-room wing was added to the hotel, doubling the hotel's guest capacity. The new section, which looks exactly like the older sections, houses a restaurant named La Canaries, in honor of the Canary Islanders who came to San Antonio in the 17th century. There is also a bar (El Capistrano) which features a flamenco guitarist, El Curro.

Reservations: (512) 225-2581 or Texas toll free (800) 292-7300. 112 College Street, San Antonio, Texas 78206.

Directions: Take any downtown exit off a major freeway leading into San Antonio. College Street is bordered by Houston and Commerce Streets and by Navarro and N. St. Mary's. For an excellent city guide and map, write San Antonio Convention and Visitor's Bureau, P.O. Box 2277, San Antonio, Texas 78298 or call (512) 226-2345.

## POINTS OF INTEREST

See the Points of Interest listed under St. Anthony's Hotel in San Antonio.

# The Plaza Nacional

*San Antonio*

The Plaza Nacional is a luxurious, six-story hotel which opened in 1979 in downtown San Antonio. The hotel structure is not historic in any way, but on the hotel property are three restored 19th-century bungalows, each representative of a particular type of early Texas home, and a 19th-century school building. The Diaz House, circa 1840, is the oldest house, showing the influence of the Alsace-Lorraine settlement in Texas. The tufa stone construction was not durable enough for exterior wear, so the outer walls were covered with stucco. The interior, however, still shows the beautiful stone walls. The Diaz House is now used for meetings and receptions.

The Elmendorf-Tylor House was built in the early 1850s by Heino Staffel. It is constructed of plaster over stone, with stucco covering the exterior walls. This house, now called Restoration Bar and Grille, is furnished with early Texas furnishings typical of the mid-19th-century period of German settlement in this area of San Antonio.

The Staffel House was also built by a member of the Staffel family and is an attractive example of a Victorian cottage. The house is constructed of brick. The Victorian design of the house is similar to the homes built in the nearby King William Historic District immediately south of the Plaza Nacional. This period was an economic and aesthetic coming-of-age in San Antonio, and many of the wealthy German settlers and prominent

Staffel House (ca. 1850)

Elmendorf-Tylor House (ca. 1850)

established families of the city built their homes in this part of San Antonio.

The German English School on the hotel grounds was also built in the mid-19th-century. It may have been the first German English school in Texas. The basic style for the hotel is sympathetic to the design of this school building, with its slanted roof tops and graceful balconies. It is used as a convention center by the hotel.

The Plaza Nacional is a top quality hotel in all its services and is decorated with attractive artwork from around the world. Many interesting places are within walking distance. HemisFair Plaza is across the street. Besides the fascinating Institute of Texan Cultures and other exhibits, it has the 622-foot Tower of The Americas, which dominates the city's skyline and has an observation deck view of the city. The tower has a bar and two restaurants. The Alamo, La Villita Historic District, and the Paseo del Rio are all a few blocks from this fine resort.

Reservations: (512) 229-1000, Telex 767-381. 555 S. Alamo Street, San Antonio, Texas 78295. $65 up for a double. Special weekend rates are sometimes available.

Directions: From IH-37/IH-35, exit on Durango, turning west. The hotel is at the intersection of Durango and S. Alamo, in downtown San Antonio.

## POINTS OF INTEREST

See the Points of Interest listed under the St. Anthony Hotel in San Antonio.

# Faust Hotel

*New Braunfels*

In 1928, 12 New Braunfels citizens built a fashionable hotel called the Travelers Hotel. The hotel's name was later changed to the Honeymoon Hotel because so many honeymoon couples stayed there. Many photographs of honeymoon couples dating back to the 1920s hang on the walls. Its rates were .50 to $2 per night.

Within a few years, bathrooms were added to each room by using closet space. Originally there had been only one bath per floor. In the 1930s, the hotel's name was changed to the Faust Hotel in honor of one of its founders, Walter Faust. In the 1950s the hotel was closed due to competition from the chain motel industry and lack of maintenance, but the dining room continued to stay open under various managements.

In 1976, Jackson, Houser, and Associates bought the Faust from Congressman Bob Krueger and family. The hotel was then remodeled. New plaster, drapes, and carpets were added. The rooms were painted and wallpaper hung. Furniture was refinished, light fixtures and ceiling fans cleaned and oiled, and brass handrails were shined. The lobby clock was rewound and the antique cash register repaired. The dining room's parquet floor was repaired and refinished, and live plants were added throughout the hotel. A hand-built teak and mahogany bar was added.

Telephones and color TVs were added to each of the

Faust Hotel

62 rooms. The rooms are somewhat plain, but quite pleasant with iron or wooden bed frames, ceiling fans, old writing tables, and lacy drapes. Some bathrooms have old porcelain fixtures and large, claw-footed tubs.

The Faust reopened for business in February 1978. It is particularly popular during the summer because of the cold, clear rivers nearby and the small town atmosphere. It is also very busy during New Braunfels' Wurstfest each November. Wurstfest offers a market place, dancing to oompah music, feasting on all kinds of sausage, strudels, and pancakes from old German recipes, canoe races, an old-fashioned beerhall, and a dachshund show, among other events.

Reservations: (512) 625-7791. 240 S. Seguin, New Braunfels, Texas 78130. $30 up for double.

Directions: New Braunfels is 35 miles northeast of San Antonio off I-35. The Faust is a block south of the town square.

## POINTS OF INTEREST

See Points of Interest listed with the Prince Solms Inn, New Braunfels.

Prince Solms Inn

# Prince Solms Inn

*New Braunfels*

The Prince Solms Inn is a small inn with eight guest rooms and two suites. The guest rooms are upstairs while the suites, lobby, and kitchen are downstairs. The basement has been converted into a popular restaurant called Wolfgang's Keller named after the German composer Wolfgang Mozart. Bill Knight, a musician and the chef, entertains guests not only with tasty meals but with his musical talents.

The inn's guest rooms are very attractively decorated in a style befitting a fine turn-of-the-century inn. The walls are covered with wallpaper of a large floral design, and the woodwork is painted a dark matching shade. Antique ceiling fans from the old Medical Arts Building in San Antonio hang from the 11-foot ceilings. There are no telephones or televisions in the rooms.

Each room has a different layout and color scheme, but all are pleasing. The rooms are small, however, and have thin walls. This is not a place you would enjoy visiting if you have small children.

The building can be described as Classic Texas Victorian. It was built in 1899 by Emilie Eggeling, a German immigrant who ran the nearby Plaza Hotel. Its exterior walls are 18 inches thick, and its ceilings are high. The first floor has 13-foot ceilings, and the second floor has 11-foot ceilings. The lumber used to construct the building came from cypress trees growing on the edge of the nearby Guadalupe River, and the soft-colored beige

Entrance and guest room

bricks were made of mud from the Guadalupe's banks. Most of the building's hardware came from Henne Hardware, still in business in New Braunfels.

The Prince Solms Inn has seen a number of owners, one being Bill Dillin, who bought the hotel in 1953 and committed himself to remodeling the interior. Dillin was an interior decorator, and whenever in the course of his work he found objects he liked, he used them in the hotel. He added 200-year-old tiles from Holland to the bar and floored the patio with the large stone blocks he bought when the Comal County Prison was torn down. He added cypress posts from the first New Braunfels woolen mill and shutters from the demolished Marlin County Courthouse.

When he sold the Prince Solms Inn to Marge Crumbaker and Betty Williams in 1977, he stipulated that there be no changes to the building's exterior. He need not have worried about Crumbaker and Williams, as they are as interested in authentically restoring the property as he was. For example, when they added air-conditioning, they told the electricians that no structural changes could be made that would alter the rooms' or halls' appearance. It was necessary to install four separate units to meet this objective. Restaurant facilities and additional parking spaces have been added, and the original brick sidewalk has been uncovered. Crumbaker and Williams had to completely furnish the hotel, since one of its former owners had taken all the lovely old furniture to San Antonio and sold it.

The Prince Solms Inn is located a short walk from the Prince Solms Park where inner tubing through a fast moving water chute down the Comal River is very popular. The Comal is a 4-mile river that runs through New Braunfels, whereas the Guadalupe travels through many towns from west of Kerrville to the Gulf Coast. Both rivers are beautiful, clear, and cold, and provide excellent recreational opportunities.

The history of this area is noteworthy, as the only

successful colony established by Germany in America developed here. A group of German noblemen decided to establish a German community in America. The Republic of Texas was chosen because it was reported to have good soil and a healthy climate. The noblemen named their immigration association the Adelsverein. Immigrants were offered the following: $240 for each household, free transportation to Texas, free land (320 acres), a log house, financing through the first crop, and a system of public services, such as churches and hospitals. The Adelsverein mistakenly assumed that huge profits would soon be made by the sale of Texas lands to help finance this venture.

The Adelsverein had acquired the old Fisher-Miller empressario grant and proposed to settle half and sell the other. Unfortunately, Fisher and Miller not only had no right to sell the land, but had already forfeited their contract. The agents for the nobles had naively assumed that all Texas lands were alike: they never saw the thin, stony soils located in Indian country. This did not become apparent until 7,000 German settlers had arrived in Texas. Prince Carl of Solms-Braunfels, one of the nobles, sought other lands nearer the coast. He chose a spectacularly beautiful site on the Guadalupe and called this township New Braunfels.

Meanwhile, German immigrants were continually unloading at the docks in Indianola. Miserable, hungry, and ill, their dreams for a better life were turning into a nightmare. A typhus epidemic began. Prince Carl of Solms-Braunfels resigned and returned to Germany, leaving Von Meusebach in charge. The Germans had to go by foot towards their new home. Due to heavy rains in East Texas, the settlers had to walk for days through mud, followed by vultures. Many immigrants died along the way, others found promising pieces of land and began farming. Finally the Germans arrived in the New Braunfels region and founded their town in 1845. The country was lovely, but farmers looked at the rocky soil with dismay and moved on to look for plowable fields nearby. There was not enough land for all the settlers, so Meusebach made a successful agreement with the Penateka Comanches to use their lands.

The farmers worked hard but did not prosper for many years. The townspeople fared better. They formed the first large financial and mercantile establishment in South Texas and originated many of the businesses in San Antonio. The German immigrants, together with the Alsatian French colonists, gave this area of Texas a certain sophistication not present elsewhere in Texas.

Reservations: (512) 625-9169. 295 East San Antonio Street, New Braunfels, Tx 78130. Rates are $40 up which includes a continental breakfast of coffee, rolls, and juice served on the patio.

Directions: The Prince Solms Inn is one block east of the town square.

## POINTS OF INTEREST

Prince Solms Park — Bring inner tubes to ride the rapids or rent them from a nearby gasoline station. Entrance fee.

Landa Park — Free picnic grounds. Paddleboats and bicycles for rent. Swimming pool, glass bottom boat.

Naeglin Bakery — Century-old bakery.

Henne Hardware — Century-old hardware store.

Gruene Hall — Claims to be Texas' oldest dance hall. Children welcome.

Sophienburg Memorial Museum — Records of the first settlers in the area.

Natural Bridge Caverns — Largest caverns in Texas. Halfway between New Braunfels and San Antonio on FM 3009.

Landmark Inn

# Landmark Inn

## Castroville

Texas parks are renowned for their innovative design and beauty, and the Parks and Wildlife Department has really done it again with the renovation of the old Landmark Inn in Castroville. The Landmark Inn complex consists of the inn, a round stone bathhouse, and a gristmill on 4-acre grounds. The complex was donated to the Texas Parks and Wildlife Department in 1974 by owner Ruth Lawler, who requested that it be preserved as a state historic site. The well-manicured grounds of the inn contain so many typical Texas trees that the area looks like a botanical garden: pecan, osage orange, fig, huisache, and cottonwood.

The Landmark Inn was built in 1849 by Caesar Monad, a French settler who came to America as a result of Henri Castro's colonization efforts in the 1840s. Henri, a French entrepreneur, received a colonization grant in 1842. Castroville was founded in 1944 as the first of four settlements in his colony. The colony, composed of settlers from the French provinces of Alsace and Lorraine, suffered from Indian attacks, epidemics, and droughts, yet Castroville survived.

Caesar Monad built a one-story stone structure to be used as his home and a general store. The building, with its plastered walls and gabled roofs covered with wood shingles, resembled the European farm houses of the Rhone Valley.

In 1853, John Vance, an Irish immigrant, bought

Caesar Monad's home and store. He added a second story to the building and a lower and upper porch. Vance used the building much like Monad did; the long portion was the family home, and the ell was used as a general store. Stagecoaches rumbled by on the old San Antonio Road, and Vance found that more and more travelers needed a room for the night. He began to rent out rooms, and eventually the building became known as the Vance Hotel.

In the 1860s the Vance family built a one-and-a-half story stone house to use as a residence, and a round bathhouse of stone with a lead lining. How refreshing that bathhouse must have been to the weary, dusty traveler. During this period, John Vance was postmaster, and the Vance Hotel served as the post office.

In 1854, Vance sold the lower part of his land to George Haass and Laurent Quintle. They built a two-story stone grist mill and an underground mill race. Soon afterward they also constructed a cotton gin.

The next family to own the hotel and mill was the Courand family, who sold it to Jordan Lawler in 1925. During the 1940s, Jordan and his sister Ruth Lawler reopened the inn as a hotel and named it the Landmark Inn. The Lawlers renovated the inn and lived in the Vance house where Miss Lawler continues to live.

The Texas Parks and Wildlife Department has repaired and painted the building, added modern bathrooms to the guest rooms, and furnished the building with lovely antique furniture. The guest rooms have not been air-conditioned, but with ceiling fans, 18-inch walls, and 11-foot ceilings, the rooms stay agreeable on impressively hot summer days. The mill has been restored, and the bathhouse has been converted into two guest rooms. The inn also houses a museum which explains the development of this French settlement and the inn. The state employees who work at the

Landmark Inn are proud of the site and will be glad to show you through or reserve you a room.

Reservations: (512) 538-2133. Box 577, Castroville, Texas 78009. $13 single, $20 double.

Directions: The Landmark Inn is located on U.S. 90, at Florence Street on the east edge of Castroville.

## POINTS OF INTEREST

French homes and bakeries throughout the town

St. Louis Catholic Church — Stone chapel built in 1869.

Lickskillet Inn

# Lickskillet Inn

*Fayetteville*

The Lickskillet Inn is located in Fayetteville, a German-Czech community which has changed very little in the last century. Most of its buildings still stand on the town square, though their function may have changed from saddle shop or opera house to grocery store or bank. Czech is still spoken in this town, the "Cradle of Czech settlement in Texas", and its Czech and German heritage can easily be seen by walking the square and looking at the store names — Bertsch's meat market, Hornak's liquor store, Chovanec's Grocery, and Onker Variety. A walking tour of the town square has been written by the inn's owner, Jeanette Donaldson, and is available free of charge in the mail box marked "Information" in front of the Lickskillet Inn.

Steve and Jeanette Donaldson bought the Lickskillet Inn in 1978. At that time it was not an inn, but a residence, the oldest home in Fayetteville, built in 1853. The home has been changed substantially from the days when it had four rooms off a hall and an open dog run to a detached kitchen.

It is now an attractive two-story frame house with four rooms for rent on the weekends. The rooms are pleasantly decorated with antique furniture, quilts, and small woodburning stoves. They have unit air-conditioners and ceiling fans which certainly come in handy in July and August. There is a shared bath close to the rooms. Scattered throughout the foyer are histor-

Four rooms to rent

ical documents for the guests to peruse. Craft items for sale are also on display.

To help guests feel at home, the refrigerator is stocked with orange juice, wine, and beer. A simple breakfast is included in the room rate, which features homemade breads and Fayetteville honey. The Donaldsons will probably hand you *The Houston Post* at breakfast and will be delighted to discuss the area's history if you are so inclined. Local history has become almost an obsession with them since they moved to Fayetteville in 1978 and bought this old home, now named after Fayetteville's old nickname, Lickskillet. The story goes that Fayetteville has always been known for its frequent public feasts, but in the 1820s or 1830s they once ran out of food and had to advise guests to "lick the skillet". So, for many years, people called it Lickskillet, Texas.

Reservations: (713) 378-2846. P.O. Box 85, Fayette Street, Fayetteville, Texas 78940. $31.50 for a double. Checks are accepted, as are Master Charge, Visa, and American Express.

Directions: Fayetteville is located at the intersection of Texas Highways 955 and 1291, north of I-10 between San Antonio and Houston. The Lickskillet Inn is one block north of the town square.

## POINTS OF INTEREST

Weekend meals at the Country Place Restaurant within walking distance of the Lickskillet Inn.

Walking tour of the century-old town square.

Country Place Hotel

# Country Place Hotel

*Fayetteville*

The Country Place Hotel in Fayetteville is an example of how much more important talent is than money where decorating is concerned. Clovis and Maryann Heimsath have used their skills in architecture and art, some elbow grease, and very little hard cash to recreate a pleasing, authentic small country inn. The Heimsaths painted or wall-papered the walls, painted the floors, and placed their own artistic creations on the walls — watercolors, oils, line drawings, and prints of their favorite buildings in Venice and Rome. They selected a variety of antique furnishings for the rooms in antique wicker, iron bed frames, gaily painted trunks, rocking baby beds, and Texas pottery. Lacy curtains and white shades cover the windows, and patchwork quilts brighten the bed.

Besides being attractive, the Country Place Hotel is in a town where crime is rare. No locks are on the doors except for a small hook and eye lock on the inside. Checking in and out is marvelously uncomplicated. When you make your reservation, find out which room you have been assigned. Upon arrival, sign the register in the antique shop and find your room upstairs. They are never locked and your name will be on a small card on the door. Before leaving, make sure you have placed your remittance in the envelope tacked to the door frame outside your room.

The Country Place Hotel's only cooling is ceiling and portable fans and good ventilation. However, during our

Elegant country living

June visit, the hotel was comfortable. None of the seven rooms have bathrooms, but there is a women's bath containing an old claw-footed tub and there is a men's restroom with a shower. Both are located down the hall from the guest rooms.

The Heimsaths bought the hotel building in 1975 to use as an office for their architectural firm. Part of the downstairs was all that was needed. It seemed a shame to let all that space go to waste, so they furnished the upstairs and began taking in guests. The remaining rooms downstairs became an antique shop, kitchen, and restaurant.

The Country Place Restaurant, serving delicious gourmet dishes, is run by Perry and Carol Thacker and is open on weekends by reservation only. From this same kitchen, guests were served in the early part of this century, many of the roomers being traveling salesmen, at that time called drummers. Other boarders were students who lived at the hotel when school was in session. The Zapp Building, as it was known when it was built in 1900, was designed to serve as a general store, but the need for lodging kept arising. It has also served as a hospital and as a photographer's studio. The old building must be rejoicing to become once again fully useful to the community.

Reservations: "On the Square", Fayetteville, Texas. (713) 378-2712 or 522-0777 if calling from Houston. Reservations can only be made between 8 a.m. and 5 p.m. $15 double, $5 for additional bed.

Directions: Fayetteville is located near La Grange, approximately halfway between Houston and Austin. The Country Place Inn is a two-story red-brick building on the town square.

## POINTS OF INTEREST
See Points of Interest for Lickskillet Inn.

Von Minden Hotel

# Von Minden Hotel

## Schulenburg

The Von Minden Hotel is being restored by the Bill and Betty Pettit family, formerly of Houston. Each member of the Pettit family contributes in some way to the hotel's operation and renovation. Grandad comes by to work on the plumbing, the sons handle most of the carpentry, with mom's fried steak the only payment. Betty and Bill paint, plaster, wallpaper, and do whatever else is necessary to get the place going.

The Von Minden is not just an old hotel, it is also an old movie theater and a pizza parlor, all in the same four-story brick building constructed in 1927. The building, which then consisted of the hotel and movie theater, was built by the Irwin and Leonida Speckel family to serve the railroad traffic. The hotel was named after Leonida's father who financed the construction. The movie theater opened in November of 1927, the hotel in May of 1928. The hotel became popular even though there were several years when the entrances were locked after the movie ended at 9:30 p.m., as there was no night clerk.

The Speckels raised their family in the Von Minden, and in fact lived there for 53 years, selling the hotel to the Pettit family in 1978.

Leonida Speckels was renowned for her housekeeping skills, and Betty Pettit now marvel at towels that are fifty years old, all worn places neatly patched with scraps. As a result of Leonida's habits, all furnishings are still in the hotel and in reasonably good condition, including the furniture which was built by the same carpenters who constructed the building. The roof had been damaged, but the floors are fine, because Leonida placed buckets under all the leaks and carefully emptied the buckets after each rain.

The hotel is now old and in need of brightening up, but that is exactly what is being done by the Pettits, one room at a time. A large renovated suite on the fourth floor is particularly attractive. A peek in the bathroom shows that even the old oak toilet seat is still in excellent condition.

Not all guest rooms have private baths, air-conditioning, or TV, but several do and more will in the future. All the rooms are still heated by steam radiators, an efficient and inexpensive method. And speaking of the hotel's mechanical operation, the Von Minden was built in a way that makes it a surprise and delight to carpenters, plumbers, and electricians. There is four feet of walk space between each floor and a foot or so between many walls to permit easy maintenance. Many of the closets have trap doors which drop down to the next floor to be used as an interior fire escape.

The hotel is interesting to tour but no more interesting than the old movie theater in one section of the building. The movie theater is still operational and shows all the latest films, but is a delightful anacronism. It has wooden seats and a stage, since the theater was designed for live productions as well as films. A cry room is located at the rear of the seating area where filmgoers can take their fretful babies and stand and watch the movie through a glass panel. There is also a small balcony with wooden benches connected to a separate movie entrance which was for black moviegoers. The section is now used by Bill Pettit for his private seating area. He can readily view the audience to make sure that all is well.

In running an old hotel, owners must be multi-talented. When Bill leaves his law office in Houston, he

drives to Schulenburg and goes to the projection room to show the films. He may have to take tickets and sell popcorn too. The projection room is filled with old equipment and movie fliers and magazines, as well as the mammoth reels now used for showing films.

The movie theater, hotel, and Momma's Pizza Parlor, added in 1981, have seen steady business lately, much of it due to the booming oil business in the area. The number of overnight guests who are there to enjoy the old building are increasing. People want to spend a night in Schulenburg's newest building, all others having been built prior to the 1920s.

Reservations: (713) 743-3493. Schulenburg, Texas 78956. Doubles $15. and up.

Directions: Schulenburg is located on the south side of I-10, approximately halfway between Houston and San Antonio.

## POINTS OF INTEREST

Monument Hill State Park — Final resting place of the men who drew the black beans of death after the Mier Expedition against Mexico. Impressive 48-foot marker of stone, bronze, and polychrome. Located 12 miles north, off U.S. 77 near La Grange.

Hempstead Inn

# Hempstead Inn

*Hempstead*

Ghazi and Anne Issa didn't think anything could get in the way of their opening a restaurant on Westheimer, Houston's restaurant row. But that was before they passed the old Peden Hotel on Highway 6 on their way through Hempstead. With a for sale sign out front, it beckoned to them irresistibly. They pulled together their money, came back to Hempstead, and bought the place.

After purchasing the hotel, the Issas spent six months remodeling it, doing most of the repair and decorating work themselves. They have neither restored the hotel to its former state, nor thoroughly modernized it. Instead, they took the middle road, cleaning and painting it, making it a comfortable, habitable inn for guests who do not require a TV, room phone, or room service. It's a quiet, hospitable lodging with reasonable rates, the kind of place travelers would like to find in every town when they are not looking for recreation, just a pleasant place to rest at day's end.

The Parks Hotel was built in 1915 by a Mrs. Parks to serve the traveling salesmen who came to Hempstead by train. In 1922 the Hermes purchased the hotel, renaming it the Peden Hotel. Why Peden? Peden was a nickname that the Hermes called each other, so they decided to give the hotel their pet name.

In 1933 the hotel was moved to face the highway instead of the train tracks, due to the change in method of transportation used by travelers. Mrs. Hermes was really the driving force behind the hotel, so after her death in 1968, the family's interest in the hotel waned, and the hotel was soon sold.

During the 1970s the hotel was sold several times, finally being purchased by the Issas, who seem willing to put enough work and money into the inn to make it go. The air-conditioned guest rooms upstairs are painted soft pleasing hues and are furnished with new-looking furniture. Few rooms have private baths, but all have a lavatory. The rooms with private bath have showers, not tubs. The public bathroom has a tub.

The Issas have added a restaurant to the inn which serves a much wider community than the inn's overnight guests. Meals consist of 10 to 12 well-seasoned vegetable dishes, four meat dishes, such as roasted Cornish game hens, grilled pork chops, beef, fried chicken, corn bread, and tasty ice cream desserts. All to be washed down with quarts of iced tea.

The Hempstead Inn is not now nor ever was anything but a plain and simple inn, yet it has served its community well. Hempstead is also a plain and simple place, with little activity except for its large fruit and vegetable stands. It gives few clues to its notorious past when it was called Six Shooter Junction. During the 1800s and early 1900s, this was a wide-open town. Men and young boys carried revolvers or sawed-off shotguns, since they never knew when they might be needed. Stagecoach and train hold-ups were not uncommon. Pity the poor drummer who came to town to hawk his wares, only to find he first had to either dance a jig or be shot when he got off the train, all for the amusement of the disorderly cowpokes.

Hempstead settlers soon found the nearby sandy soil a watermelon grower's dream. During the late 19th century, Hempstead came to be called the Watermelon Capital of the World when watermelon fanciers around the country found that no melon could match those from Hempstead. During those days as many as 1800 box car loads of melons were shipped in a single season. Today, people from surrounding towns and cities are quite willing to drive to Hempstead and pick up a sweet red or gold-meated melon. They also drive over for the fine country cooking at the Hempstead Inn.

Reservations: (713) 826-6379. 435 10th Street, Hempstead, Texas 77445. $30 for a double.

Directions: Hempstead is 60 miles northwest of Houston on Texas Highway 290. The Hempstead Inn is located in Hempstead on Highway 290.

## POINTS OF INTEREST

Fruit and vegetable stands throughout the city, with watermelon and corn the area's specialties.

Country eating

The Toland House

# The Toland House

*Chappel Hill*

The Toland House charms you as soon as you open the front door to the cozy parlor and notice the fresh flowers, the cut glass dish of chocolate kisses, and the note which says to help yourself to wine, cheese, and crackers in the kitchen. Another note gives instructions for breakfast, which can be put on a tray and taken up to the room or to the front or back porch. The *Houston Post* will be on the front porch in the morning.

Part of the hotel's charm is its innkeeper Eve Knapp. She is the one who has put out the fresh flowers, the candy, and the notes. She lives close by and will be over to meet the guests, introduce people, and keep the conversation going at a lively pace. Then she will probably depart for her weekly poker game.

The Toland House has only four bedrooms. The downstairs room is the Honeymoon Suite with an antique four-poster bed so high there is a stepping stool to climb up to it. The Rooster Room is the only other room with a double bed. The reason behind its name shall not be given away except to say that there is a guaranteed wake up. The fourth room is the only one with a bathroom in the room. The Rooster Room and the third room share a bathroom, but it is no problem to do so. The third and fourth rooms are as yet unnamed.

The Toland House was built in 1912 by Mrs. Mary Hale Toland, widow of one of the town's first physicians. Dr. Toland's office was moved to the rear of the property to make room for the two-story building which was attached to the house as the kitchen and store room. Mrs.

Toland served good food, and one of the boarders, formerly a music teacher at Chappell Hill Female College, often gathered people around the parlor piano for a musical evening. Mrs. Toland died in 1931, and the hotel became a private residence until purchased in October, 1978, by Mr. and Mrs. Thomas A. Bullock, Sr. In the spring of 1980, refurbishing was complete and the structure was once again a hotel.

Chappell Hill was begun in 1847 by Jacob and Mary Haller and named for pioneer settler Robert Wooding Chappell. It soon became the educational, cultural, and Methodism center of Stephen F. Austin's second colony. The Men's and Women's College began in 1850 or 1852 and became part of the Methodist Church in 1854. In 1856 it divided into Soule University for the men and Chappell Hill Female College for the women. A museum is now on the site of the college a short walk down Popular Street from the hotel.

Next to the museum is the United Methodist Church, first built in 1853, blown down in the 1900 storm, and then rebuilt in 1901 by Henry C. Brandt, a local contractor. The tools he used to build the church are in the museum next door. The acoustics are supposed to be perfect. The walls, floor, and ceiling are of wood finished with hot oil, which has never required refinishing. The ceiling is constructed in the shape of a Maltese cross. Each stained glass window is a memorial to a person or group.

The Providence Baptist Church is a short walk down Main Street. It was first built in 1853, later destroyed by storm, and the present building erected in 1873. There are tours available of many of the other buildings in the area.

The Toland House has been decorated to give an atmosphere of warmth and hospitality. Eve wants it to feel like someone's grandmother's house and indeed it does. She tries to put out the American flag faithfully each day, and it is a nice welcoming touch to see it waving in front of the hotel. The rooms are spacious, being at least 11 by 12 feet with 10-foot ceilings, and sunny with windows on all three sides. Ceilings on the first floor are even higher. There is central air and heat with separate controls in each room, and also ceiling fans. The beds are antique with new comfortable mattresses. The walls are cream colored with brown woodwork. Each room is different and nicely decorated.

When we were at The Toland House all the other guests were there to go to the Round Top Festival, which is not far from Chappell Hill. There is a lot to see in the Chappell Hill area, or a weekend could easily be spent at the hotel just sitting around reading a good book.

Reservations: Weekdays after 4:30—(713) 622-8386. Weekends (713) 836-5747 or (713) 836-0973. P.O. Box 207. Main at Popular, Chappell Hill, Texas 77426. $25 single, $30 double. Rooms are available on weekends or during the week by special arrangement.

Directions: U.S. 90 toward Brenham, right on F.M. 1155 which becomes Main St., to Main at Poplar. Hotel on right corner.

### POINTS OF INTEREST

Chappell Hill Scarecrow Festival in October. Shouldn't miss this unique event.

Chappell Hill original downtown, down the street from the hotel.

Chappell Hill Home Tours — Contact the Chamber of Commerce for information. (713) 836-6382 P.O. Box 113, Chappell Hill, Tx 77426

Bluebonnet Antique Show and Sale in April. Contact the Chamber of Commerce.

Round Top Music Festival, Round Top, and Winedale. Henkel Square, P.O. Box 82, Round Top, Tx 78954 (713) 249-3308. Music Institute at

United Methodist Church

Festival Hill, (713) 249-3129. Winedale Historical Center, P.O. Box 11, (713) 278-3530

Washington-on-the-Brazos State Historical Park, where the founders of the Republic of Texas signed the Declaration of Independence from Mexico in 1836. 15 miles from the hotel on F.M. 1155. Museum and historical buildings. Park open 8:00—dusk daily. Buildings open 10-5 daily, March — Labor Day and Wed. — Sunday, Sept.-Feb. P.O. Box 317, Washington, Tx 77880. (713) 878-2461

Blue Bell Creameries — Tours at 10 a.m. Tuesday and Thursday. Loop 577 in Brenham. P.O. Box 650, Brenham, Tx 77833 (713) 836-7977

Chappell Hill Tour — Includes creamery tour, historic homes, Washington-on-the-Brazos, and antique shops. (713) 836-6717.

Peaceable Kingdom — classes in organic gardening, pottery, food, health, solar energy, and basketweaving and a store with some of their products. Ask Eve for directions.

190

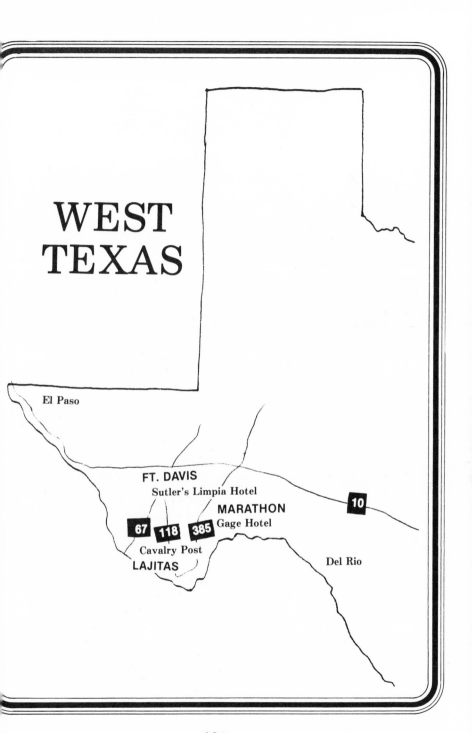

WEST
TEXAS

El Paso

FT. DAVIS
Sutler's Limpia Hotel
MARATHON
67 118 385 Gage Hotel
10
Cavalry Post
LAJITAS
Del Rio

Gage Hotel

# Gage Hotel

## Marathon

In the early part of the 20th century, Marathon was a bustling ranching center of West Texas. Cattle buyers came to Marathon by train to meet ranchers and inspect their herds. If a sale was made, the rancher would drive his 6,000 to 10,000 head of cattle to the Marathon stockyards, where they stayed until loaded on train cars and shipped to San Antonio or Ft. Worth. There was only one snag in this otherwise smooth operation; the cattlemen and buyers had no place to meet to haggle over prices and close a deal. The cattlemen often talked of building a hotel to serve this purpose, but somehow it never got done. So Alfred Gage, a rancher owning 500,000 acres of West Texas land, decided to take on the project, and in 1926 the construction of the Gage began.

Mr. Gage chose the architectural firm of Trost and Trost to design the hotel. This firm also designed the University of Texas at El Paso and the Paisano Hotel in Marfa. With its tan brick and Spanish-style arched doorways, the hotel fits in well with the surrounding landscape. The Gage is two stories high with most of its 20 guest rooms upstairs. In its early days, the downstairs contained the lobby, the office used for negotiating cattle prices, and a barbershop. It was the largest building in town, the only one with indoor plumbing.

The Gage opened April 1, 1927, and the cattlemen found the hotel most useful for conducting business. Tourists also began to drop by on their way through this

Old Ranch Hotel

sparsely populated land with few accommodations. The Gage became a popular place for town dances, and as Mrs. Frank Wedin, the 85-year-old town historian told us, "When you holler 'dance' in West Texas, everybody comes". The hotel also became home base for paleontologists from the Smithsonian Institute who dug fossils from nearby mountains for more than forty years. And in 1928, Zane Grey stayed at the Gage while he was studying the land and customs of the West for his next novel.

Eventually, however, the Gage began to deteriorate. Each remodeling seemed to mean lower ceilings, another coat of paint, and more linoleum over the lovely oak floors. This elegant building seemed on its way to oblivion when it was rescued in 1978 by J.P. Bryan of Houston, who owns ranch land near Marathon. He has spared no expense in returning the Gage to its 1927 appearance.

Carpenters have not only spent months stripping and staining the doors, transoms, and floors, they have also been kept busy building furniture to match that of early Texas. A wash basin has been added to each guest room without a bath, and a women's shower room has been added, as the hotel had not been designed with women in mind. The Gage was most definitely a man's hotel. The new Gage has a masculine atmosphere, too. Maybe it's the ranch style doors, or the heavy trunks in the rooms, the absence of bric-a-brac, or the stuffed elk and bobcat. Or perhaps, if a building is designed well, its essential character will be hard to disguise.

The hotel's opening day in March of 1981 included a dance, and sure enough, people from all over West Texas were willing to drive to Marathon so they could waltz and two-step. The wind shrieked and blew unmercifully as it can only do on the plains, yet it would take more than that to stop the dance and barbecue.

The new owner is hoping to make a success of his hotel by offering more than a nice hotel and restaurant to his guests. He wants to assist them in locating the type of entertainment they are looking for. If it is a raft trip, or horseback rides, or tours of Big Bend National Park, he can arrange it. The stark desert landscape surrounding Marathon should attract plenty of city dwellers who want to spend time in this land of silence and stillness.

Reservations: (713) 236-2969. Avenue C North and Highway 90, Marathon, Texas 78942. The Gage was temporarily closed as of January 1982. It should reopen soon.

Directions: Marathon is located on U.S. 90, 330 miles west of San Antonio. The Gage is in Marathon, on U.S. 90.

## POINTS OF INTEREST

Big Bend National Park — 708,221 acres of spectacular mountain and desert scenery. Park headquarters are approximately 80 miles south via U.S. 385.

Black Gap Wildlife Management Area — 100,000 acres devoted to the study and development of management practices for the protection of native wildlife. Visitors welcome. 55 miles south via U.S. 385 and Ranch Road 2627.

Amtrak ride — The Sunset Limited, which runs between New Orleans and Los Angeles, stops in nearby Alpine. The ride on Amtrak between Houston and Alpine is a most delightful way to see West Texas. The Gage furnishes pick-up service from the train station.

# Limpia Hotel

*Fort Davis*

The Limpia Hotel was built in 1912 by a group of local merchants known as the Union Trading Company. The 12-room, two-story, pink building was constructed to serve the many tourists who traveled to Fort Davis on the Southern Pacific, eager to reach the cool, pleasant summer climate of mile-high Fort Davis. The first floor of the hotel housed a dining room and kitchen, a drug store, and the town's doctor.

The Limpia continued serving guests until 1953 when it was damaged by fire. J.D. Duncan bought the hotel, repaired it, and converted the upstairs into apartments. The downstairs housed the offices of Harvard University School of Astronomy. Duncan eventually sold the hotel, then rebought it in 1971, this time with historic preservation in mind. Noting the gradual deterioration of many of the fine old buildings and the town's flagging economy, he decided to teach a unit on building restoration and preservation to his high school civics class at Fort Davis High School. The class's enthusiasm for what they learned spread to their parents who began to restore the downtown area. J.C. also became enthusiastic and decided to purchase the old Limpia Hotel, named after nearby Limpia stream. Limpia means clear or clean in Spanish.

J.C. and his wife Isabelle added a balcony to the second floor and enclosed the open porch, to which they added comfortable rocking chairs and pots of bright red geraniums, begonias, and lacy ferns. The guest rooms are attractively furnished with oak furniture, light blue cotton eyelet drapes and bedspreads, and a blue rose

Limpia Hotel

carpet. The rooms are large, 18 feet square, not counting the bathrooms. The ten and a half foot ceilings covered with pressed tin add to the spacious feeling. Though the rooms' style is reminiscent of the past, many concessions have been made to accommodate modern-day travelers; cable TV, telephones, air-conditioning, and modern plumbing.

Next door to the Limpia is a craft shop and a restaurant called The Boarding House. These are also owned by the Duncans. The restaurant serves good steaks, including chicken fried steak, and tasty homemade pies.

The Limpia Hotel is in Fort Davis, named after the fort established there in 1854 in an attempt to keep the Apaches and Comanches under control. The fort, now part of the Fort Davis National Monument, is an interesting museum, with officers quarters, cannons, army uniforms, medical equipment, and photographs on display. This was one of the places where the U.S. Army experimented with using camels as pack animals for traversing the U.S. deserts. The experiment ended with the outbreak of the Civil War.

The McDonald Observatory is near Fort Davis. A tour of the observatory and new visitors center can make a morning pass quickly. All in all, Fort Davis is a pleasant and attractive place to visit, and not the least of these attractions is the Limpia Hotel.

Reservations: (915) 426-3237. P.O. Box 822, Fort Davis, Texas 79734. Single $20. Double $30 to $40. No pets. No credit cards accepted.

Directions: The Limpia is located on the town square, on State Highway 118.

## POINTS OF INTEREST

Old Fort Davis — Fort used for Indian fighting, now serves as a museum.

Fort Davis National Park — Scenic campground and picnic site. Motel accommodations are available at the Indian lodge.

McDonald Observatory — Welcomes visitors.

# The Cavalry Post

*Lajitas*

The Cavalry Post is not an old hotel, but is interesting as a replica of an old army post built to keep peace on the U.S/Mexico border. The Cavalry Post is built on the foundation of the army barracks which once served General John J. Pershing in his attempts to keep Pancho Villa under control. After a raid by Pancho Villa, General Pershing would pursue Villa through the wastelands of northern Mexico, Villa on horseback, Pershing in his Cadillac.

Lodgers at the Cavalry Post live in considerably more comfort than did those early army men. The rooms are spacious, attractively decorated, and air-conditioned, no small luxury in a country where the temperature climbs to 115°F in the summer.

If you like having a kitchen, you could stay in one of the cabins, built in the old style of adobe brick. Basic grocery supplies can be bought at the Trading Post, a popular border store for more than a century. The goats at the store will be glad to share your potato chips and cold drinks.

The Cavalry Post is part of a larger complex called Lajitas on the Rio Grande, all built by a Houston real estate developer, Walter Mischer. There are curio shops, a saloon, and a restaurant that serves piquant border fare; flour tortillas, refried beans, Tampico steak. River rafting trips can be arranged at Lajitas, as can horseback riding, either a short ride or an overnight pack

Cabin at The Cavalry Post

trip. A landing strip accommodates those who arrive in small aircraft.

The Cavalry Post is a relaxing place to stay, sitting on the cabin's front porch, admiring the vast blue skies and stark scenery of West Texas, counting the brilliant stars, or watching the wild burros grazing in the moonlight at night. It is a pleasant place to return to after exploring the magnificent desert park, Big Bend National Park, 20 miles east of the Cavalry Post.

Reservations: (915) 371-2471. P.O. Box 18, Terlingua, Texas 79852. $30 (double), or $50 up for cabins

Directions: The Cavalry Post is located in Lajitas, Texas which can be reached by taking F.M. 170 from Presidio, or Texas 118 from Alpine, or U.S. 385 from Marathon. We took Amtrak from Houston to Alpine, then rented a car from the Big Bend Motor Company in Alpine.

## POINTS OF INTEREST

Big Bend National Park — 708,221 acres of desert wilderness, including deep gorges formed by the Rio Grande River, and the Chisos Mountains. The park has many well-developed hiking trails, an information center, lodging and camping areas, and horseback riding. The Park has over 1,100 plant species, and wildlife is just as varied: coyotes, deer, javelinas, skunks, rabbits, beaver, mountain lion. The high season for this area is April when all types of cacti and other desert plants bloom profusely.

Terlingua — Once a mining town, now a ghost town of adobe buildings. Scene of World Championship Chili Cook-Off in the fall.

Editor's Note: The Cavalry Post Motel was destroyed by fire on August 14, 1982.

A Rio Grande Valley citrus grove.

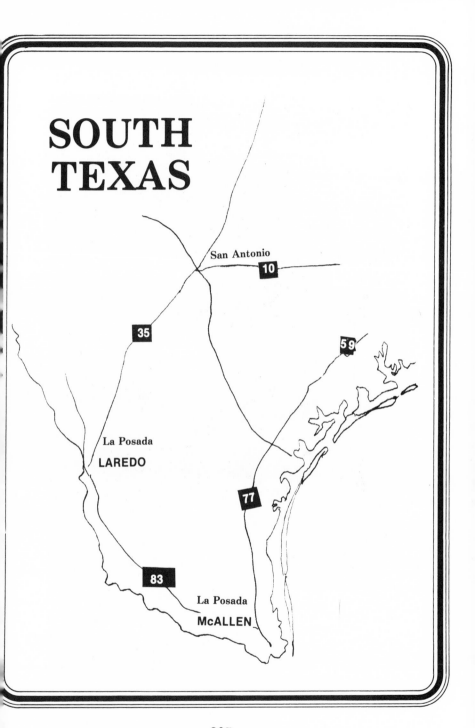

# SOUTH TEXAS

San Antonio

**10**

**35**

**59**

La Posada
**LAREDO**

**77**

**83**

La Posada
**McALLEN**

La Posada — McAllen

# La Posada

## McAllen

La Posada Motor Hotel is an ideal destination for travelers who would like to experience the food, music, and atmosphere of Mexico but aren't yet ready to strike out for the interior, to haggle with taxi drivers and vendors, to meet head on with people of a different language and culture. La Posada has all that is needed to create the festive air of Mexico — a refreshing pool, tile-lined and surrounded by violet and red bougainvillea vines, fruit-bearing banana trees, and coconut palms. A mariachi band plays all the tourists' old favorites — Malagueña, Cielito Lindo, Quizas, as guests lie by the pool sipping margaritas or pina coladas. The hotel restaurant serves a variety of Mexican dishes, although the visitors from Mexico prefer, of course, to order prime rib and baked potatoes.

La Posada is a reasonably priced hotel in comparison with other full-service hotels. It has the unobtrusive type of service which meets the needs of those who expect someone to carry their bags but leaves alone those who feel uncomfortable having personal services performed for them.

None of the guest rooms are small, and the parlor bedrooms are particularly spacious, having plenty of room for two double beds, a sofa, a dining table, refrigerator, and bar. The decorating scheme is not particularly innovative; it is what always comes to mind when furnishings are described as Spanish — red

Pleasant patio

Modern facilities

bedspreads, dark wood furniture, white walls, and exposed ceiling beams. However, the view from the six-foot windows is pleasant of the patio, well kept lawns, enormous fig trees, and Mexican fan palms.

The hotel's two bridal suites are most unusual, maybe a bit much for anyone who cannot imagine a pink shag carpet. Each suite is tri-level, each level connected by a spiral staircase, with the bedroom on the second floor. Pink beads serve as the doorway between the bedroom and bath. The top level has a sofa and color TV and a fine view of McAllen.

The exterior of La Posada is classical Spanish, with white stucco finish, red tile roof and floors, archways, and twin towers. The three-story building encircles a patio which contains the swimming pool. The front view of the hotel is greatly enhanced by the presence of a magnificent African sausage tree, which is covered with what appear to be vines but which are actually flower-bearing tendrils. The tree is native to Mozambique, where it is held sacred and its fruit used to treat skin diseases.

La Posada is a reincarnation of the old Casa del Palmas hotel built on this site in 1918. In 1905, the railroad came to McAllen, causing a growth spurt, as did the introduction of irrigation, which made vegetable farming possible. An even greater growth occurred in 1916, when 12,000 soldiers were stationed in McAllen to quell border raids by bandits. After the arrival of the troops, the need for a business and social center became apparent, so a group of businessmen built the Casa de Palmas in 1918.

The Casa de Palmas did indeed meet the Rio Grande Valley's need for a place to meet socially and to talk business. In 1919 it also served as the town's refuge from a severe hurricane.

In 1971, the Casa de Palmas was purchased by Pan-Tex Hotel Corporation which renamed it La Posada, the Resting Place. The hotel was upgraded and prepared for a grand opening in 1974. A few days before opening day, lightning struck the hotel, and a fire started. The streets were flooded, so that fire trucks could not arrive in time to prevent the lovely old hotel from burning to the ground.

The hotel owners didn't spend much time worrying about their loss. They simply rebuilt the hotel. Only the foundation and some floors were salvageable, but the new hotel opened a year later. Even though La Posada is new, it has the same romantic atmosphere and warmth of an old hotel. Perhaps some of Casa de Palmas spirit has wafted up through the foundation. La Posada in the moonlight is pure magic.

Reservations: (800) 528-1234 (Texas toll free) or (512) 686-5411. 100 N. Main, McAllen, 78501. $50 up for a double. Larger suites, including honeymoon suites, are available.

Directions: McAllen is one of the southernmost points in Texas. After reaching McAllen, turn north off Business 83 onto N. Main Street.

### POINTS OF INTEREST

Reynosa, Mexico — shopping for Mexican handicrafts, restaurants specializing in wild game dishes. La Posada provides a shuttle bus to Reynosa.

Gladys Porter Zoo in Brownsville, Texas. — Beautiful zoo filled with exotic animals and plants, in a garden setting with few bars or cages.

Miles of grapefruit and orange tree groves.

210

# La Posada

## Laredo

La Posada (the resting place) is a large, attractive hotel conveniently located only a block from the old international bridge that links Laredo and Nuevo Laredo. The hotel is built around a lovely tropical courtyard containing a large tile pool surrounded by lounge chairs and tables with umbrellas. Poolside rooms open onto the walkway or a balcony overlooking the pool. Bougainvillea is in bloom everywhere. In the early evening, a marimba band plays here.

La Posada has done an excellent job of incorporating existing buildings into their hotel plan. The old Laredo High School, built in 1916, became the hotel's offices, reception area, club, restaurants, and ballroom. The ballroom with its 20-foot ceilings was once the school's auditorium. The old building was a superb choice for forming the central part of a Spanish-style hotel. It is stone, brick, and adobe, with one-foot-thick walls.

Also located on the hotel property is the capitol building of the short-lived Republic of the Rio Grande. It is a rock, adobe, and wood building constructed around 1835. The grounds also contain the old San Agustin Church convent, built in 1767. La Posada recently acquired the Bruni Home on the block to the west, which it will restore and use as a restaurant called the Tack Room in honor of horse racing in the Laredo area.

La Posada is located in a city with an interesting history. While the rest of Texas has seen the flags of six

La Posada — Laredo

nations flown above it, Laredo has seen seven. In 1836, Texas declared its independence from Mexico, but Laredo was actually governed by Mexico until 1856. During this period, Antonio Canales and other Federalists from Mexico and Texas were in opposition to the reigning Mexican Centralists who had discarded the Mexican Constitution of 1824. They established the Republic of the Rio Grande which encompassed northern Mexico and Texas south of the Nueces River. Canales named Laredo as the republic's capital in January, 1840. Headquarters was a small, one-story building.

The Centralists' army arrived in Laredo in March, 1840, and crushed the republic without a fight. Federalists leader Antonio Zapata was captured and killed. Federalists counterattacked and recaptured Laredo and other towns, but at Saltillo, Mexico, they were outnumbered. The Federalists deserted Canales, and he surrendered to Arista. The Republic had existed only 283 days.

Reservations: (512) 722-1701. 1000 Zaragoza, Laredo, Tx 78040. $42-47—single, $50-57—double, $125-175—suite.

Directions: Follow the signs in Laredo to the historical district or to the old international bridge. The hotel is two blocks from the bridge on Zaragoza St., which runs directly in front of the bridge.

### POINTS OF INTEREST

Lake Casa Blanca — recreational activities, including golf

Horse racing in Laredo and Nuevo Laredo

Historical District, San Augstin Plaza, directly in front of the hotel. Bell in San Agustin Church made in early 1700s.

Spanish style hotel

Good Neighbors 4-hour tour of Los Dos Laredos, 5900C San Bernardo, Laredo, Tx 78041 (512) 724-7054

Mexico

Washington's Birthday, celebrated in such a way as you might never have seen before. First celebration here in 1899.

Exponex and Diez y Seis (Mexican Independence Day) festivities in September.

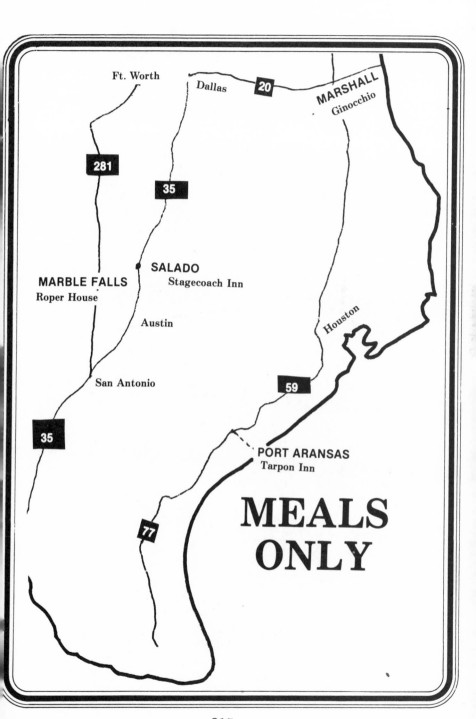

Ft. Worth

Dallas

**20**

**MARSHALL**
Ginocchio

**281**

**35**

**SALADO**
Stagecoach Inn

**MARBLE FALLS**
Roper House

Austin

Houston

San Antonio

**59**

**35**

**PORT ARANSAS**
Tarpon Inn

**77**

# MEALS ONLY

Roper House

*Photo courtesy of the Roper House*

# Roper House

*Marble Falls*

When the stagecoach rolled into Marble Falls, it often stopped at the home of Elizabeth and George Roper to request water, supplies, and an overnight room for a passenger. The Ropers eventually decided that they had given away enough free service, so in 1888 they built the Roper Hotel.

The train soon overshadowed the stagecoach as a major means of transportation, but that didn't slow business down at the Roper Hotel. Business boomed as Marble Falls became a popular resort area. The dry climate was reputed to be healthy, and many suffering from malaria contracted on the Gulf Coast came to Marble Falls to stave off another attack. The town also called itself the "Manufacturing Center of the Southwest". Granite from local quarries was transported by rail to build the state capitol, and aferry went back and forth across the Colorado River.

Mrs. Roper's good cooking was well-known. Not only train travelers, but local farmers would come to the Roper Hotel, the farmers arriving by mule or ox-drawn wagon. After all, early Texas was hardly famous for its food. Most inns served three meals a day consisting of cornbread, bacon, and black coffee. Another attraction of the Roper House was the steamship the Ropers kept on Lake Marble Falls (now called Lake LBJ) so that guests could enjoy a leisurely ride.

When Mr. Roper died in 1912, Mrs. Roper continued

Dining at the Roper Hotel.

to run the hotel, but she found it too much of a handful and sold it to W.F. Smith in 1926. The Smith family ran the hotel until the 1950s. From that time on it was sold several times and had begun to look worn and tired.

Don and Michelle Gunn purchased the hotel in 1978, intending to fully restore it as an inn and fine restaurant. They gathered information on the hotel's history in preparation for having the building listed on the National Register of Historic Places, which was achieved in 1980. Researching the hotel's past was not difficult, since Michelle had grown up nearby and had visited the hotel many times as a child.

As the Gunns planned the hotel's restoration, they felt that the building was more suited to being a restaurant than a hotel. They removed all interior walls and exposed brick on the outer walls. They installed new hardwood and built a new stairway with balustrades matching those on the outside balcony.

The Gunns have restored the exterior meticulously. They reviewed old photographs, talked to a granddaughter of the Ropers who was raised in the hotel, and sent samples of paint and mortar to a lab to duplicate the original construction and materials as closely as possible. It was discovered that the tan bricks were made nearby from clay from the banks of the Colorado River. Five missing chimneys were replaced. Four of them had been used for wood-burning stoves, but are now nonfunctional. The fifth is connected to a working fireplace on the ground floor.

The concrete front porch was replaced with a wooden one and contains two of the original porch chairs. A granite wall in front of the building has been reconstructed with the original stones. Structurally the building has been improved so much that it is now more sound than when it was built.

Operated by Ron and Merianne Wininger, The Roper House restaurant offers an unhurried and friendly atmosphere. Upon entering the building, guests first notice the rich colors of the wallpapers and fabrics. Ceiling fans, light fixtures, antique chairs, etched and stained glass, and other accent pieces are reminiscent of the turn of the century building.

The entire building is used for restaurant facilities, with the two main dining areas on the first and second floors. Banquets and private parties can also be scheduled. Guests may enjoy the amenities on the shaded east patio made of native stone and surrounded by a wooden pickett fence.

The evening menu, which changes somewhat from week to week, features regional as well as continental French cuisine. Selections include poultry, seafood, Provini veal, steaks, and prime ribs. A full service bar is available. However, Burnet County is dry, so guests can obtain a $2 temporary membership to buy liquor or make selections off the wine list.

A light lunch menu is served in a casual atmosphere Tuesday through Sunday.

Reservations call 693-5561.

Directions: Marble Falls is located on Texas Highway 281, forty miles northwest of Austin. The Roper House is on Texas 281 and Third Street.

## POINTS OF INTEREST

Granite Mountain — Large dome of high-quality red and pink granite. Quarrying began in the 1880s for construction of the Texas Capitol building. The mountain is a half-mile west off Ranch Road 1431.

Highland lakes — This area has a series of seven large lakes, famous for fishing, boating, swimming.

# Stagecoach Inn

*Salado*

The grounds of the Stagecoach Inn have long been a popular resting and watering place, perhaps due to its large oak trees and nearby creek. It was first used by Indian tribes who camped here and left messages on a large pecan tree behind where the inn now stands. Early Texas settlers camped here in their wearying journey across the land. The Chisholm Trail intersected this area, as did the Overland Stage Line route from Little Rock, Arkansas, to San Antonio. It was only fitting that an overnight lodging be established.

The inn was built around 1850 as a one-story wood structure which had to be expanded to two stories within a few years due to increased travel. It was then called the Shady Villa because of the magnificent trees on the property. It quickly filled with guests such as old-time cattle baron Shanghai Pierce and other cattle traders driving vast herds up the Chisholm Trail to the Kansas stockyards. Stagecoach passengers also kept the inn busy, as did military men such as General Custer. Colonel Robert E. Lee had come to Salado once to quell an Indian uprising and again in an effort to re-introduce camels into Texas. In 1861, General Sam Houston, then governor of Texas, stood on the inn's long porch and made his famous but unpopular anti-secession speech.

Notable law-abiding citizens were not the only guests, however, as legend says that the Youngers and the James Brothers roomed here. Infamous bank robber

Stagecoach Inn

Sam Bass hid in the cave behind the inn the night before he was shot down by the Texas Rangers.

When the stagecoach days ended, deterioration set in, but through the efforts of various individuals, the inn is still standing. It is now a restaurant which serves lunch and dinner seven days a week. There is a set price for the meal, which includes several courses and iced tea or coffee. Meals consist of a choice of baked ham, stuffed shrimp, prime rib, pork chops, fresh vegetables, corn bread, and a dessert. The food at the inn is not as good as its earlier reputation but it is still pleasant, and obviously quite popular. It is wise to make reservations, particularly on weekends.

The Stagecoach Inn is on the grounds of a motel of the same name, so there is a place to stay the night if you choose to do so. A bright red stagecoach sits in front of the motel, commemorating bygone days.

Reservations: (817) 947-5111. This is the number to call to reach either the motel or the Stagecoach Inn restaurant.

Directions: The Stagecoach Inn motel is located in Salado and can easily be seen from U.S. 35. Salado is forty miles northeast of Austin on U.S. 35.

### POINTS OF INTEREST

Antique shops

Central Texas Area Museum — Depicts area's history with documents, exhibits.

Tarpon Inn

# *Tarpon Inn*

## *Port Aransas*

The Tarpon Inn is a pleasant two-story frame build-ing with wide porches which run the length of the build-ing. Its lobby walls are covered with 7000 tarpon scales bearing the autographs of such fishermen as President Franklin Roosevelt, who stayed in suite 29.

The inn was built in 1886 with materials from Civil War barracks. It burned in 1900. Two new buildings were erected that year. In 1919, a hurricane and tidal wave destroyed the larger building and damaged the smaller one, which was repaired and became the restau-rant. A second building was built in 1925, which is the one now used as a hotel.

The hotel was renovated in 1956, and unfortunately is in need of further renovation. The rooms are small, but could be quite charming with some brightening touches such as paint, new lamps, and window coverings. On the porch outside the rooms are plenty of comfortable old chairs.

One outstanding redeeming feature of the hotel is its restaurant, open Thursday through Sunday evenings part of the year. Situated behind the hotel, it is attrac-tively but plainly furnished as befits a seaside restau-rant. The food is well prepared and the service is friend-ly. The stuffed shrimp and frozen lime pie are particular-ly good. The restaurant is also a pleasant place to go for a drink. You can sit inside or on the long screened-in porch.

During the fall, the Tarpon Inn is popular with duck

hunters. The inn can arrange for guides and can cook and serve wildfowl or dress it for freezing. Breakfast and box lunches are available. The Port Aransas area is not just popular for duck hunters, however. It's also a favorite place for surf and deep-sea fishing. Beach and pier catches include redfish, speckled and sand trout, sheepshead, flounder, croakers, skipjack, and drum. Charter boats are available for bay and deep-sea fishing. Offshore species include sailfish, marlin, kingfish, mackerel, ling, pompano, bonito, red snapper, and tarpon. In July, anglers from all over the U.S. come to Port Aransas to compete in the Deep Sea Round Up.

Another major attraction of this area is the Aransas Wildlife Refuge, the winter home of over 35 species of migratory waterfowl. During the fall, as many as 35,000 Canadian geese are at the refuge at one time. Mixed flocks of pintails, mallards, and teal have reached a count of 120,000. Wild turkey can be seen here during all seasons. The Wildlife Refuge is particularly famous as the only winter home of the almost extinct whooping crane. Yearly the cranes make their 2,500-mile trip between their summer home in Canada and this winter resort. Their wild trumpeting cry, which can be heard for two miles, sounds across the marshes in mid-October announcing their arrival.

The refuge is about 30 miles from Port Aransas, near Austwell. You can drive through the refuge in an hour, or spend all day there. The visitor's information center has free maps and brochures and a slide show on the whooping crane. There are picnic grounds, trails of varying lengths to lakes, marshes, or ocean points, and a lookout tower. On the trails it's possible to uncover deer, alligators, armadillos, raccoons, javelinas, and rabbits.

Buy or rent binoculars for this trip. Bird guidebooks, such as *Birds of North America* or *A Field Guide to the Birds of Texas* might also come in handy. Even if you've never considered yourself a bird fancier you may leave

Padre Island morning.

the refuge wanting to know more about the snowy egrets or the great blue herons.

Reservations: (512) 749-5555. Call for restaurant hours.

### POINTS OF INTEREST

Mustang Island State Park. Primitive area of 3,474 acres on the Gulf of Mexico. Camping, fishing, and swimming permitted, but no facilities provided. Located 14 miles south of Port Aransas on Park Road 53.

Party boats provide bay and deep-sea fishing.

A nearby Tyler rose garden.

## POINTS OF INTEREST

Caddo Lake State Park

Franks Musuem — Special exhibit of more than 800 rare and antique dolls.

Harrison County Historical Society Museum — Remodeled former county courthouse depicts history of Marshall and of Harrison County.

# Ginocchio Hotel

## Marshall

The old Ginocchio Hotel in Marshall is certainly one of the loveliest hotels built to serve railway passengers, in this case the Texas and Pacific Railway. It is also one of the largest of the railway hotels in Texas, with 40 guest rooms, a ballroom, lobby cafe, small shops, and a large dining room. With ten sets of double doors, the entire front of the building opened when the train was in the station to admit as many as 400 hungry passengers eager for the delicious and hearty 25¢ lunch which had to be served quickly and efficiently.

The Ginocchio Hotel was built in 1893 by Charles A. Ginocchio, who came to Marshall in the early 1870s. He operated a restaurant and saloon located about 60 feet east of the present hotel building. It was in this restaurant that Maurice Barrymore was shot in the arm in an argument concerning the reputation of a female member of the theatre troupe.

The Ginocchio is a building built to last. Sturdy construction was necessary to withstand the vibration of the train which passed within a few feet of the hotel. The foundation was built of hand sawed native iron stone, with walls three feet thick in the basement. The brick walls are 20 inches thick, and all interior framework is heart pine and cypress.

The hotel was also built for aesthetic appeal. The interior of the building is trimmed with nearly a mile of curly pine wainscot of exceptional beauty. This uniquely patterned pine is all that survives of a stand of timber discovered in the 1880s in Vernon Parish, Louisiana. There were only 1,500 acres of this timber in the stand, and after it was cut by a milling operation, no new growth ever developed. The wood is almost all clear pine, as hard as a pine knot. So hard, in fact, that it could only be finished in the Texas and Pacific Railway shops at Marshall where the special machinery and talented craftsmen were located. The railway shop workers were used to complicated carpentry projects, since the elaborate woodwork in the Pullmans and lounge cars had to be precise to withstand all the swaying and jolting that train cars were subject to.

The interior of the hotel is also embellished by a magnificent staircase that reaches to the third floor. Midway up the staircase is a balcony which served as the hotel manager's office. From this vantage point, he could survey all the comings and goings and keep an eye on the cash register. His rifle lay nearby in the hotel's wilder days.

The hotel's guest rooms have been closed for years, but the restaurant has remained in business. During 1981 the restaurant was closed for remodeling. It should reopen early in 1982. We hope it will still serve Sam Litzenberg's notable cheesecake.

Reservations: Contact the Visitors Convention Center for information (214) 935-3583. The Ginocchio and the convention center are located at 700 N. Washington, Marshall, Texas 75670.

Directions: The Ginocchio is four blocks north of U.S. 80, on the corner of Ginocchio and Washington.